7 7 7

Revelation's Was, Is, & Is To Come

Carolyn L. Mason

© Copyright 2018 Carolyn L. Mason.
All rights reserved. No portion of this book may be reproduced, stored in a retrieval system, or transmitted in any form or by any means – electronic, mechanical, photocopy, recording, scanning, or any other – except for brief quotations in critical reviews or articles, without the prior written permissions of the publisher and author.

Published by Carolyn L. Mason
carolynlmason@suddenlink.net

All scripture quotations King James Version are taken from www.Biblegateway.com. No permission necessary. Public domain.
Scripture references are taken from The King James Study Bible, ©Copyright 1988, U.S.A., Thomas Nelson, Inc. previously by Liberty University.

The World Book Encyclopedia, ©Copyright 1989, U.S.A. by World Book, Inc. Wikipedia, The Free Encyclopedia. No permission necessary. Public domain.

Strong's Concordance KJV is taken from www.Biblehub.com. No permission necessary. Public domain.
The New Strong's Exhaustive Concordance of the Bible, ©Copyright 1990, U.S.A, by Thomas Nelson Publishers.

Webster's Third New International Dictionary, ©Copyright 1981, U.S.A. by Merriam Webster Inc.

Irwin Baxter's End of the Age Television Program, United States of America found in the bible. No permission necessary. Public domain.

The Mayfield Clinic is taken from (https://www.mayfieldclinic.com/PE-natBrain.htm). No permission necessary. Public domain.

Library of Congress Cataloguing-in-Publication Data is on file with the Library of Congress.

ISBN 978-1-7324537-0-8

Edited by Carolyn L. Mason

Printed in the United States of America.
2018 – First Edition

The internet addresses, email addresses, and phone numbers in this book are accurate at the time of publication. They are provided as a resource. The publisher does not endorse them or vouch for their content or permanence.

Cover and Design by Carolyn L. Mason

Dedication

This book is dedicated to God, the Father, Jesus-God the Son, and God the Holy Spirit and to my deceased parents, grandparents, family, spiritual mothers, saints, and to all of those unselfish under-shepherds, deceased and living. Each of you has helped me to know and fall in love with the Blessed Godhead. To all of you, I say thank you from the depths of my heart and soul. Thanks for the contributions you have made in my spiritual walk with the Lord. It really does take a village!

Contents

The Purpose	8
In the Beginning	12
The Holy Trinity – The Triune God	12
The Fall of Lucifer / Ice Age	16
The Six Days of Creation	22
Day 1	23
Day 2	24
Day 3	24
Day 4	24
Day 5	25
Day 6	26
Leviticus 23 - The Feasts of the Lord	28
Passover	29
Unleavened Bread	29
First Fruits	29
Pentecost	29
Trumpets	30
Day of Atonement	34
Tabernacles or Booths	34
Exodus 33 – Show Me Your Glory	36
Genesis 4 - The Purpose of Cain and Abel's Offerings (Body and Blood of Jesus)	42
Chapter One	52
Chapter Two	56
The Church Of Ephesus	56
The Church In Smyrna	57
The Church In Pergamos	58

The Church In Thyatira	*59*
Chapter Three	61
The Church In Sardis	*61*
The Church In Philadelphia	*62*
The Church Of The Laodiceans	*62*
Chapter Four	64
Declaring The End From The Beginning	*64*
The Heavenly Vision	*66*
Chapter Five	73
The Heavenly Vision Continues	*73*
Chapter Six	77
The Seven Seals (Was)	*77*
1st *Seal – Satan (Rider on White Horse)*	79
2nd *Seal – Sword (War)*	82
3rd *Seal – Famine (Hunger)*	91
4th *Seal – Death and Hell*	95
5th *seal – Martyrs*	101
6th *seal - Pentecost*	103
Chapter Seven	106
144,000 Sealed Prior to the Tribulation & Great Tribulation	*106*
Multitude From the Great Tribulation in White Robes	*109*
Chapter Eight	110
7th *seal- Pentecost*	110
The Day the Church Began	116
The Seven Trumpets (Is)	*124*
1st *Trumpet*	125

2nd Trumpet	125
3rd Trumpet	125
4th Trumpet	126
Chapter Nine	127
5th Trumpet	127
6th Trumpet	131
Chapter Ten	133
Chapter Eleven	137
Two Witnesses	137
7th Trumpet	145
Chapter Twelve	151
Woman and the Dragon	*151*
Chapter Thirteen	159
The First Beast out of the Sea (The Antichrist)	*159*
Daniel 7– Three Beasts	*161*
The Second Beast out of the Earth (False Prophet)	*166*
The Mark of the Beast	*166*
Chapter Fourteen	176
The Lamb of God and the 144,000	*176*
Three Angels Warnings of Soon Judgments to Come	*177*
Harvesting the Earth at the Second Advent & the Great Winepress	*179*
Chapter Fifteen	182
Chapter Sixteen	184
The Seven Vials (Is to Come)	*184*
1st Vial	184
2nd Vial	185

3rd Vial	185
4th Vial	185
5th Vial	185
6th Vial	185
7th Vial	186
Chapter Seventeen	189
Nebuchadnezzar's Image & Daniel's 70 Weeks	*191*
The Tower of Babel	*203*
Mystery Babylon	*205*
Daniel 7 - The Fourth Beast - The Headquarters of the United Nations	*208*
Chapter Eighteen	221
Babylon, the Great Is Fallen	*221*
Chapter Nineteen	228
Alleluia Praises in Heaven	*228*
Second Coming of Christ	*229*
Chapter Twenty	234
Chapter Twenty One	237
New Heaven and a New Earth	*237*
New Jerusalem	*238*
Chapter Twenty Two	241
Conclusion	244
Prayer of Salvation	253
Prayer for the Baptism with the Holy Ghost	254

THE PURPOSE

The purpose of writing this book is:

- **For all men to fall in love with God, the Father and His Son, Jesus.**

- **To let all mankind know of God's great agape love for His man creation and the depths and means to which He will go to prove His love.**

- **To let the atheist know that there is a self-existent, in the beginning, God.**

- **To let the sinner know of God's redeeming love through Jesus, the Christ (God incarnate).**

- **To let the redeemed know of His ever-present, abiding, sustaining, and relatability love.**

The Purpose

- **To make known the 7-fold blessings of Jesus' Birth, Life, Death, Burial, Resurrection, Ascension, and Second Coming (Advent).**

- **To make known the hidden truths that God had hidden for us and wants us to know.**

His initial purpose was to dwell among and fellowship with His man creation forever without sin, death, and Satan. And guess what? He will, in the end, have just what He intended in the beginning, in the Millennium, and in the New Heavens and Earth. God loves us so much that He created us in His image and likeness.

This book will also let you know the following:

- <u>**God prepared the perfect earth environment. He planted His man creation in the Garden of Eden and gave them dominion over all of His works.**</u>

Genesis 1:28-30 says, "And God blessed them, and God said unto them, be fruitful, and multiply, and replenish the earth, and subdue it: and have dominion over the fish of the sea, and over the fowl of the air, and over every living thing that moveth upon the earth. And God said, Behold, I have given you every herb bearing seed, which is upon the face of all the earth, and every tree, in the which is the fruit of a tree yielding seed; to you it shall be for meat. And to every beast of the earth, and to every fowl of the air, and to every thing that creepeth upon the earth, wherein there is life, I have given every green herb for meat: and it was so."

- **He took on the form of a man in order to redeem man.**

Philippians 2:6-11 says, "Who, being in the form of God, thought it not robbery to be equal with God: But made Himself of no reputation, and took upon Him the form of a servant, and was made in the likeness of men: And being found in fashion as a man, He humbled Himself, and became obedient unto death, even the death of the cross. Wherefore God also hath highly exalted Him, and given Him a name which is above every name: That at the name of Jesus every knee should bow, of things in heaven, and things in earth, and things under the earth; And that every tongue should confess that Jesus Christ is Lord, to the glory of God the Father."

- **He assures us that nothing and no one can separate us from His love.**

Romans 8:35, 38-39 says, "Who shall separate us from the love of Christ? Shall tribulation, or distress, or persecution, or famine, or nakedness, or peril, or sword? For I am persuaded, that neither death, nor life, nor angels, nor principalities, nor powers, nor things present, nor things to come, nor height, nor depth, nor any other creature, shall be able to separate us from the love of God, which is in Christ Jesus our Lord."

- **He understands and can relate to us in ways no other god can.**

The Purpose

Hebrews 4:14-16 says, "Seeing then that we have a great High Priest, that is passed into the heavens, Jesus the Son of God, let us hold fast our profession. For we have not an High Priest which cannot be touched with the feeling of our infirmities; but was in all points tempted like as we are, yet without sin. Let us therefore come boldly unto the throne of grace, that we may obtain mercy, and find grace to help in time of need."

IN THE BEGINNING

The Holy Trinity – The Triune God

First John 5:7 says, *"For there are three that bear record in heaven, the Father, the Word, and the Holy Ghost: and these three are One."* They are One. There is only One God. God, the Father, is manifested in Three Persons also known as the Godhead. The Father is a Spirit (John 4:24). The Word of God is Spirit (John 6:63). The Holy Spirit is Spirit. The Word of God became flesh in the person of Jesus. He is still the Father (John 14:8-11). God, the Father, took His Spirit (The Word) and placed Him in the womb of a virgin, named Mary, and called Him Jesus, Immanuel, God with us (Luke 1:26-38; Matthew 1:18-25; Isaiah 7:14).

In the Beginning

John 1:1-5, 14 says, *"In the beginning was the Word, and the Word was with God, and the Word was God. The <u>Same</u> was in the beginning with God. All things were made by Him; and without Him was not any thing made that was made. In Him was Life; and the Life was the Light of men. And the Light shineth in darkness; and the darkness comprehended it not... And the Word was made flesh, and dwelt among us, (and we beheld His Glory, the Glory as of the only begotten of the Father,) full of Grace and Truth."* Jesus is the image of the invisible God. He is the firstborn of every creature (Colossians 1:15-19). Jesus, also called the last Adam, is a quickening, Life-Giving Spirit (1st Corinthians 15:45-47). Jesus, the Word made flesh, is the source of all life (Hebrews 11:3; Colossians 1:15-17; Ecclesiastes 3:19-20).

Jesus is described in Revelation 1:14-15, *"His head and His hairs were white like wool, as white as snow; and His eyes were as a flame of fire; And His feet like unto fine brass, as if they burned in a furnace; and His voice as the sound of many waters."* And in Revelation 19:12-13 when it says, *"His eyes were as a flame of fire, and on His head were many crowns; and He had a name written, that no man knew, but He Himself. And He was clothed with vesture dipped in blood: and <u>His Name is called The Word of God</u>."* Jesus is also described in 1st Timothy 6:16. *"Who only hath immortality, dwelling in the Light which no man can approach unto; Whom no man hath seen, nor can see: to Whom be honour and power everlasting. Amen"* **(Daniel 7:9-14, 22; Revelation 4:2-3).**

In the Beginning

In Jesus' pre-incarnate state, the Old Testament refers to Him sometimes as the Angel of the Lord (Exodus 3:1-4) and Melchizedek, King of Salem (Genesis chapter 14; Hebrews chapters 5-7). Pre-incarnate means He existed before being born of a woman. He says in John 17:5 *"And now, O Father, glorify Thou Me with Thine Own Self with the Glory which I had with Thee before the world was."* And in John the 14th chapter verses 8-11 the scripture says, *"Philip saith unto Him, Lord, show us the Father, and it sufficeth us. Jesus saith unto him, Have I been so long time with you, and yet hast thou not known Me, Philip? <u>he that hath seen Me hath seen the Father</u>; and how sayest thou then, Show us the Father? Believest thou not that I am in the Father, and the Father in Me? The words that I speak unto you I speak not of Myself: but the Father that dwelleth in Me, He doeth the works. Believe Me that I am in the Father, and the Father in Me: or else believe Me for the very works' sake."*

Jesus was very much the Word of God in the flesh. When He died on the cross and His Spirit (the Word of God) hit the Bosom of Abraham, the veil in the temple rent in two from top to bottom. The earth quaked, the rocks rent, and the graves were opened (Matthew 27:50-53). All of these things occurred before His body (temple) was taken off of the cross and placed in Joseph of Arimathea's borrowed tomb. Satan forgot that the spirit and soul of a man lives forever. The devil said to Jesus several years prior to Jesus' crucifixion, *"If Thou be the Son of God, cast Thyself down: for it is written, He* *shall give His angels charge concerning thee: and in their hands they shall bear thee up, lest at any time thou dash thy foot against a stone"* (Matthew 4:4-6; Luke 4:9-11). Only the body, which is mortal, perishes and returns to dust (Genesis 3:19, Matthew 10:28). When Jesus rose from the grave three days later, many not all, the Old Testament saints sleep in the Bosom of Abraham rose also (Matthew 27:50-54). Therefore, at Jesus' Second Advent, every eye will see Him as Jesus, the Word of God, in His glorified body whether living, at the time of His return, or returning with Him.

In the Beginning

The Fall of Lucifer / Ice Age

Genesis 1:1-2 (KJV)

¹In the beginning God created the heaven and the earth.
²And the earth was without form, and void; and darkness was upon the face of the deep. And the Spirit of God moved upon the face of the waters.

The bible begins with Genesis chapter one verse one telling us that in the beginning, God created the heaven(s) and the earth. The heavens refer to the original sky and the original celestial area consisting of the sun, moon, and stars before the recreated earth. The second verse tells us that the earth was without form and void. Darkness was upon the face of the deep. Then, the Spirit of God moved upon the face of the waters.

As we read these verses we wonder what happened between verses one and two. Was the earth really created without form or void? Is verse two describing the state of the earth in verse one? Did something happen between the verses? And if something happened, what happened? To get the answers to these questions, we have to go to Jeremiah chapter 4 verses 23-31.

"I beheld the earth, and, lo, it was without form, and void; and the heavens, and they had no light. I beheld the mountains, and, lo, they trembled, and all the hills moved lightly. I beheld, and, lo, there was no man, and all the birds of the heavens were fled. I beheld, and, lo, the fruitful place was a wilderness, and all the cities thereof

In the Beginning

were broken down at the presence of the Lord, and by His fierce anger. For thus hath the Lord said, The whole land shall be desolate; yet will I not make a full end. For this shall the earth mourn, and the heavens above be black; because I have spoken it, I have purposed it, and will not repent, neither will I turn back from it. The whole city shall flee for the noise of the horsemen and bowmen; they shall go into thickets, and climb up upon the rocks: every city shall be forsaken, and not a man dwell therein. And when thou art spoiled, what wilt thou do? Though thou clothest thyself with crimson, though thou deckest thee with ornaments of gold, though thou rentest thy face with painting, in vain shalt thou make thyself fair; thy lovers will despise thee, they will seek thy life. For I have heard a voice as of a woman in travail, and the anguish as of her that bringeth forth her first child, the voice of the daughter of Zion, that bewaileth herself, that spreadeth her hands, saying, Woe is me now! for my soul is wearied because of murderers."

From these scriptures we learn the conditions of the earth. The Lord God allows Jeremiah to see the earth and that it was without form and void. The heavens had no light. Then he tells us that he saw the mountains trembling and all of the hills moved lightly. He lets us know that there was no man and all the birds of the heavens were fled. The fruitful place was a wilderness and all the cities were broken down at the presence of the Lord and by His fierce anger. *The Lord said, "The whole land shall be desolate; yet will I not make a full end. For this shall the earth mourn, and the heavens above be black; because I have spoken it, I have purposed it, and will not repent; neither will I turn back from it. The whole city shall flee for the noise of the horsemen and bowmen; they shall go into thickets, and climb up upon the rocks: every city shall be forsaken, and not a man dwell therein. And when thou art spoiled, what wilt thou do? Though thou clothest thyself with crimson, though thou deckest thee with ornaments of gold, though thou rentest thy face with painting, in vain shalt thou make thyself fair; thy lovers will despise thee, they will seek thy life. For I have heard a voice as of a woman in travail, and the anguish as of her that bringeth forth her first child, the voice of the daughter of Zion, that bewaileth herself, that spreadeth her hands, saying, Woe is me now! For my soul is wearied because of murderers."*

From these verses in Jeremiah chapter 4, we are able to receive the answers to our questions regarding what happened in Genesis between verses one and two. We learn that in verse one of Genesis that God created the heavens and earth. The earth was a fruitful place with mountains, hills, birds, cities, and no man. We also learn that verse two of Genesis is a result of Almighty God's fierce anger. Jeremiah tells us that the Lord spoke and the whole land became desolate. Job tells us that it was from God's shaking the earth. Job 9:5-7 says, *"Which removeth the mountains, and they know not: which overturneth them in His anger. Which shaketh the earth out of her place, and the pillars thereof tremble. Which commandeth the sun, and it riseth not; and sealeth up the stars."* We know that there was a shaking because Jeremiah tells us that the mountains were trembling and all of the hills moved lightly.

Therefore, God did not completely abolish the heavens and earth but wanted the earth to mourn and the heavens above to be black. The heavens and earth were made void of light. Darkness was everywhere causing the waters of heaven and earth to freeze resulting in an Ice Age. For example, when a partial or total eclipse of the sun occurs, the earth's atmospheric temperature drops speedily within a few minutes and darkness is covering that part of the earth. These waters were frozen according to Job 38:29-30, *"Out of whose womb came the ice? and the hoary frost of heaven, who hath gendered it? The waters are hid as with a stone, and the face of the deep is frozen."*

We also learn that His anger was targeted at a certain individual that is not a human. The man was not created until the sixth day of the recreated heavens and earth. He tells this individual about a woman in travail bringing forth her first child, the voice of the daughter of Zion (Jerusalem). This woman bewails herself and spreads her hands saying, *"Woe is me now! For my soul is wearied because of murderers."* The individual being spoken to is Lucifer, also known as Satan, who provoked the Lord's anger. The "as of a woman" is the nation of Israel. Micah 4:10-11 tells us that, *"Be in pain, and labour to bring forth, O daughter of Zion, like a woman in travail: for now shalt thou go forth out of the city, and thou shalt dwell in the field, and thou shalt go even to Babylon; there shalt thou be*

In the Beginning

delivered; there the Lord shall redeem thee from the hand of thine enemies. Now also many nations are gathered against thee, that say, Let her be defiled, and let our eye look upon Zion." This woman, the nation of Israel, is given hope that the Lord will deliver her. This deliverance for the entire nation of Israel will occur at Jesus' Second Advent.

What did Lucifer (Satan) do to cause God's fierce anger? To get the answers to this question is found in Isaiah the 14th chapter. *"How art thou fallen from heaven, O Lucifer, son of the morning! how art thou cut down to the ground, which didst weaken the nations! For thou hast said in thine heart, I will ascend into heaven, I will exalt my throne above the stars of God: I will sit also upon the mount of the congregation, in the sides of the north: I will ascend above the heights of the clouds; I will be like the Most High. Yet thou shalt be brought down to hell, to the sides of the pit. They that see thee shall narrowly look upon thee, and consider thee, saying, Is this man that made the earth to tremble, that did shake kingdoms; That made the world as a wilderness, and destroyed the cities thereof; that opened not the house of his prisoners?"*

We learn from these verses that Lucifer, also known as Satan, thought in his heart that he would ascend into the third heaven, where God Almighty resides and sit also upon the mount of the congregation, in the sides of the north and be like the Most High. Ezekiel 28:13-17 confirms that Satan was in Eden, the garden of God, and that he was an anointed cherub that covered. He was perfect in his ways from the day that he was created until iniquity was found in him. His heart was lifted up because of his beauty. He corrupted his wisdom because of his brightness (splendor). Therefore, God cast him to the ground. Jesus confirms this event in Luke the 10th chapter and the 18th verse when He told his disciples that He beheld Satan as lightning fall from heaven. Because of Lucifer's fall, the earth was made to tremble and kingdoms did shake. Lucifer fell, at this time, by himself because of the iniquity in his heart. God did not give him a chance to utter the words in his heart. This fallen angel provoked the Lord God to wrath. Therefore, the world became a wilderness and the cities destroyed. The horsemen and bowmen mentioned in this chapter are angels.

This event mentioned in Jeremiah the 4th chapter could not have occurred at any other time in history because the earth/world would never be a wilderness (uninhabited by humans) again. The next time the earth/world will be destroyed is by fire after Christ's thousand-year millennial reign. Second Peter 3:7 says, *"But the heavens and the earth, which are now, by the same word are kept in store, reserved unto fire against the day of judgment and perdition of ungodly men."*

THE SIX DAYS OF CREATION

In Isaiah 45:18, the Lord tells us that, *"For thus saith the Lord that created the heavens; God Himself that formed the earth and made it; He hath established it, He created it not in vain, He formed it to be inhabited: I am the Lord; and there is none else."* The scripture also tells us in Hebrews chapter 11 that *"Through faith we understand that the worlds were framed by the Word of God, so that things which are seen were not made of things which do appear."*

This brings us to the six days of creation. They were literally twenty-four hours days because the scripture refers to each day as the evening and the morning. Exodus 20:11 says, *"For in six days the Lord made heaven and earth, the sea, and all that in them is, and rested the seventh day: wherefore the Lord blessed the Sabbath day, and hallowed it."* And in Exodus 31:17

which says, *"... for in six days the Lord made heaven and earth, and on the seventh day He rested, and was refreshed."* Jesus asked in John 11:9, "Are there not twelve hours in a day?"

In Job chapter 38:4-41, God asked Job, "Where was he when God laid the foundations of the earth?" He continues to question Job in regards to Job's knowledge of creation. We learn in this chapter that the earth has been around for some years because He chides Job about Job's pre-eminence and lifespan. *"Knowest thou it, because thou wast then born? Or because the number of thy days is great?"* John tells us in John 1:1-5, *"In the beginning was the Word, and the Word was with God, and the Word was God. The same was in the beginning with God. All things were made by Him; and without Him was not any thing made that was made. In Him was Life; and the Life was the Light of men. And the Light shineth in darkness; and the darkness comprehended it not."* John tells us in this chapter about creation's history and Creator.

Day 1

God said, *"Let there be light: and there was light."* God called the light Day and the darkness He called Night. This light source is not generated by the sun or moon since they were not created until day 4. God called His work good. The evening and the morning were the first day.

The Six Days of Creation

Day 2

God said, *"Let there be a firmament in the midst of the waters, and let it divide the waters from the waters."* This firmament is called sky (the 1st heaven). God called His work good. The evening and the morning were the second day.

Day 3

God said, *"Let the waters under the heaven be gathered together unto one place, and let the dry land appear: and it was so."* The waters under the heaven were gathered together in one place and the dry land appeared. God called the dry land earth and the gathering together of the waters He called seas. God said, *"Let the earth bring forth grass, the herb yielding seed, and the fruit tree yielding fruit after his kind, whose seed is in itself, upon the earth: and it was so."* God spoke all vegetation into existence consisting of the grass, the herb yielding seed, the fruit tree yielding fruit after its kind whose seed is in itself. God called His work good. The evening and the morning were the third day.

Day 4

God said, *"Let there be lights in the firmament of the heaven to divide the day from the night; and let them be for signs, and for seasons, and for days, and years: And let them be for lights in the firmament of the heaven to*

The Six Days of Creation

give light upon the earth: and it was so," God spoke the sun and the moon into existence and they were created to divide the day from the night. They were also created for signs, seasons, days, and years. They will give light upon the earth. The sun is the greater light to rule the day and the moon is the lesser light to rule the night. The scripture says, "He made the stars also." This leads us to believe that they were already created. Job 9:7 says, *"Which commandeth the sun, and it riseth not; and sealeth up the stars."* In the new heaven and the new earth, we will have no need of the sun and the moon, but the stars will be there (Revelation 21:1). The area in which the sun, the moon, and the stars reside is known as the second heaven (1st Corinthians 15:40-41). God called His work good. The evening and the morning were the fourth day.

Day 5

God said, *"Let the waters bring forth abundantly the moving creature that hath life, and fowl that may fly above the earth in the open firmament of heaven."* God spoke to the waters to bring forth abundantly the moving creature, after their kind that has life, and every winged fowl, after its kind, to fly above the earth in the open firmament of heaven. God blessed them, saying, *"Be fruitful, and multiply, and fill the waters in the seas, and let fowl multiply in the earth."* God called His work good. The evening and the morning were the fifth day.

The Six Days of Creation

Day 6

God said, *"Let the earth bring forth the living creature after his kind, cattle, and creeping thing, and beast of the earth after his kind: and it was so."* God spoke to the earth and made it bring forth the beast of the earth after its kind, the cattle after their kind, and everything that creeps upon the earth after its kind and God saw that it was good.

Then God said, *"Let Us make man in Our image, after Our likeness: and let them have dominion over the fish of the sea, and over the fowl of the air, and over the cattle, and over all the earth, and over every creeping thing that creepeth upon the earth."* So God created man in His image and in the image of God created He him (them). They are spirit beings possessing a soul and living in a physical body. He created them male and female (Genesis 5:1-2). God blessed them and said, *"Be fruitful, and multiply, and replenish the earth, and subdue it: and have dominion over the fish of the sea, and over the fowl of the air, and over every living thing that moveth upon the earth."* God said, *"Behold, I have given you every herb bearing seed, which is upon the face of all the earth, and every tree, in the which is the fruit of a tree yielding seed; to you it shall be for meat. And to every beast of the earth, and to every fowl of the air, and to everything that creepeth upon the earth, wherein there is life, I have given every green herb for meat."* And it was so. God saw everything that He had made and beheld it was very good. The evening and the morning were the sixth day.

The Six Days of Creation

On day 1 through day 6, God spoke the earth, as we know, into existence from a restorative (recreated) position. He made man in His image and likeness. God (Elohim, the Word of God) spoke and formed man from the dust of the earth and breathed into his nostrils the breath of life and man became a living soul. A man had never existed before in the earth. He created the man (Adam) first and then He created the female (Eve) from the rib of the man (Adam). Adam named every living creature. Everything that God created was created in their mature adult state capable of bearing seed of itself. Therefore, which came first? Is it the chicken or the egg? The chicken, of course, was created first.

LEVITICUS 23 - THE FEASTS OF THE LORD

The Feasts of the Lord are God's calendar of events or preplanned timeline of events that will occur (Leviticus 23:2, 44). They are exact to date in occurrence and succession. The Feasts of the Lord are Passover, Unleavened Bread, First Fruits, Pentecost or Weeks, Trumpets, Day of Atonement, and Tabernacles or Booths.

The first three feasts are referred to by some as Passover and occurred in the spring (1st Corinthians 15:3-4). Jesus has already fulfilled all of these spring feasts by His death, burial, and resurrection. Trumpets, Day of Atonement, and Tabernacles (Booths) are harvest feasts that occur in the fall.

Leviticus 23 - The Feasts of the Lord

Passover

In Passover, Jesus is our sinless Passover Lamb to Whom our sins were imputed and died for our sins. It is figuratively of His death (1st Peter 1:18-19). He was chosen by God. He was judged or declared twice by Pilate to be sinless who found no fault in Him (Luke 23:4, 14). Yet, He was crucified to take away all of our sins (past, present, and future) (Romans 8:1-11).

Unleavened Bread

Unleavened Bread is Jesus (the Bread of Life), Who knew no sin, was buried in the heart of the earth (at this time in the Bosom of Abraham) (Matthew 12:40; 1st Corinthians 5:6-8). This feast lasts for seven days and spans the time period of the Feast of First Fruits.

First Fruits

First Fruits is figurative of Jesus' bodily resurrection from the grave three days after His death. He is the First Fruit of them who were sleep (dead) in the grave (1st Corinthians 15:14-23). He is the first person to rise from the grave with a glorified body. Believers are now considered blameless or justified as if they never sinned (Colossians 1:20-23).

Pentecost

Pentecost is the initial outpouring of the Holy Spirit into the earth in Acts chapter 2. It is a spring feast occurring fifty days after First Fruits. *(See Chapter 8 The 7th Seal For Further Discussion.)*

Leviticus 23 - The Feasts of the Lord

Trumpets

Trumpets is a memorial of the blowing of trumpets and is a holy convocation symbolizing the harvesting of souls, believing Jews and Gentiles (Leviticus 23:24). The scripture tells us in Matthew 9:35-38, *"And Jesus went about all the cities and villages, teaching in their synagogues, and preaching the gospel of the kingdom, and healing every sickness and every disease among the people. But when He saw the multitudes, He was moved with compassion on them, because they fainted, and were scattered abroad, as sheep having no shepherd. Then saith He unto His disciples, <u>The harvest truly is plenteous, but the labourers are few; Pray ye therefore the Lord of the harvest, that He will send forth labourers into His harvest.</u>"* Men are consistently be harvested daily by believing and receiving Jesus, the Christ, as Lord and Savior. Just like there were three raptures of these individuals named Enoch, Elijah, and Jesus, there will be several major harvests of saints (believers) called the first resurrection. And they are as follows: some Old Testament saints at Christ's resurrection, the remaining Old Testament saints, the New Testaments saints at His Coming in the air, and the Great Tribulations saints at His Second Advent (1st Corinthians 15:35-49; John 6:40, Daniel 12:2, and Isaiah 26:19).

Some martyred Old Testament saints have already been harvested (Revelation 6:9-11). They were harvested at the resurrection of Jesus. *(See Chapter 6, The Fifth Seal.)*

The New Testaments saints will be harvested at the catching away of the saints called the rapture of the

Leviticus 23 - The Feasts of the Lord

church. *(See Chapter 11, The Seventh Trumpet and 1st Thessalonians 4:16-17.)*

The Great Tribulations saints will be harvested at the Second Advent of Jesus Christ, The Word of God (Revelation 7:14, 20:4-5).

The second resurrection is the resurrection of the dead which are those who rejected the gospel of Jesus Christ. *(See Revelation Chapter 20:11-15.)*

We are currently in the fall harvest feast called the Feast of Trumpets which occurs after the Feast of Pentecost. You ask, "What happened to the four months gap between the Feast of Pentecost and the Feast of Trumpets?" Jesus tells us in John 4:34-35, *"Jesus saith unto them, My meat is to do the will of Him that sent Me, and to finish His work. Say not ye, There are yet four months, and then cometh harvest? Behold, I say unto you, Lift up your eyes, and look on the fields; for they are white already to harvest."*

Since the Feast is Trumpets is a harvest feast, then we as His disciples are commissioned by our Lord to be laborers in our Father's vineyard and *"Go ye therefore, and teach all nations, baptizing them in the name of the Father, and of the Son, and of the Holy Ghost: Teaching them to observe all things whatsoever I have commanded you: and, lo, I am with you always, even unto the end of the world. Amen"* (Matthew 28:16-20; Mark 16:14-20).

The scripture lets us know in Galatians 2:27-29, *"For as many of you as have been baptized into Christ have put on Christ. There is neither Jew nor Greek, there is neither bond nor free, there is neither male nor female: for ye are all one in Christ Jesus. And if ye be Christ's, then are ye*

Leviticus 23 - The Feasts of the Lord

Abraham's seed, and heirs according to the promise." Therefore, God does call women into His service. There were women included in the Great Commission when He said, "Go." When He poured out His Holy Spirit into the earth, cloven (divided) tongues did not skip over the women, but fell on all of them. There is a verse that used to confuse me and now I have revelation knowledge of that verse. The verse is found in 1st Timothy 2:15 which says, *"Notwithstanding she shall be saved in childbearing, if they continue in faith and charity and holiness with sobriety."* Christ has redeemed the woman from the curse in Genesis via His birth. By Him being born and fashioned in a man's body, crucified, and resurrected, He redeemed us from all curses. We are all one in Christ, male and female (1st Peter 3:7). Therefore, let us love one another and provoke one another to love and to follow Christ and His teachings (Matthew 28:20).

Trumpets are also a memorial of the blowing of trumpets. A memorial is something that causes a certain person or an event to be remembered. In honor of Jesus' death, we partake of the Lord's Supper (Communion). First Corinthians 11:24-26 says, *"And when He had given thanks, He brake it, and said, Take, eat: this is My body, which is broken for you: this do in remembrance of Me. After the same manner also He took the cup, when He had supped, saying, this cup is the new testament in My blood: this do ye, as oft as ye drink it, in remembrance of Me. For as often as ye eat this bread, and drink this cup, ye do shew the Lord's death till He come."* We honor Jesus by our love for Him when we

Leviticus 23 - The Feasts of the Lord

carry out His Great Commission in Matthew 28:18-20, *"And Jesus came and spake unto them, saying, All power is given unto Me in heaven and in earth. Go ye therefore, and teach all nations, baptizing them in the name of the Father, and of the Son, and of the Holy Ghost: Teaching them to observe all things whatsoever I have commanded you: and, lo, I am with you always, even unto the end of the world. Amen."*

Trumpets are also a holy convocation. Convocation means the call to assemble together for a special purpose. Not only do we assemble together for Communion, but we also assemble together for worship. Hebrews 10:24-25 tell us that *"And let us consider one another to provoke unto love and to good works: Not forsaking the assembling of ourselves together, as the manner of some is; but exhorting one another: and so much the more, as ye see the day approaching."* This is exactly what our Lord Jesus did with Peter in John 21:15-17 which says, *"So when they had dined, Jesus saith to Simon Peter, Simon, son of Jonas, lovest thou Me more than these? He saith unto Him, Yea, Lord; Thou knowest that I love Thee. He saith unto him, <u>Feed my lambs</u>. He saith to him again the second time, Simon, son of Jonas, lovest thou Me? He saith unto Him, Yea, Lord; Thou knowest that I love Thee. He saith unto him, <u>Feed My sheep</u>. He saith unto him the third time, Simon, son of Jonas, lovest thou Me? Peter was grieved because He said unto him the third time, Lovest thou Me? And he said unto Him, Lord, Thou knowest all things; Thou knowest that I love Thee. Jesus saith unto him, <u>Feed My sheep</u>."*

Leviticus 23 - The Feasts of the Lord

We know that the disciples were told to assemble in Jerusalem in Acts 1:4 which reads, *"And, being assembled together with them, commanded them that they should not depart from Jerusalem, but wait for the Promise of the Father, which, saith He, ye have heard of Me."* On the day of Pentecost, the Holy Spirit was poured out into the earth. Peter preached to the multitudes and three thousand souls were added to the church and baptized (Acts 2:41). Also, in the book of Acts, the disciples assembled on the first day of the week to break bread and worship (Acts 20:7).

Day of Atonement

The Day of Atonement is the Second Advent of Jesus in which all of Jacob (Israel) will be harvested at that time (Isaiah 63:1-6; Matthew 23:39; John 19:37; and Revelation Chapters 19 and 20). The Antichrist and the False Prophet will be thrown into the Lake of Fire (Revelation 19:20). The Great Supper of the Lamb will occur at that time which is the defeat of the armies that gathered together against the nation of Israel to fight. Christ will defeat these enemies with the sword of His mouth (Revelation 19:17-21). This is a supper you *do not* want to be invited to because the attendees will be the main course and feasted upon by the fowls of the air. Satan will be chained in a bottomless pit prior to Christ's Millennial reign (Revelation 20:1-3).

Tabernacles or Booths

Tabernacles or Booths is figurative of Christ's Millennial reign in which all saints, Jews, and Gentiles, will tabernacle with Him in peace, from Satan's powers, for a thousand years prior to the New Heaven and Earth (New Jerusalem). Satan will be chained in a bottomless pit during this time period (Revelation 20:1-3; Isaiah 14:15-20). The Marriage Supper of the Lamb will occur at this time (Revelation 19:7-9). Jesus said in Matthew 26:29, *"But I say unto you, I will not drink henceforth of this fruit of the vine, until that day when I drink it new with you in My Father's kingdom"* (Mark 14:24-25). This kingdom will occur in the current earth. It is not our permanent home with Jesus, but our temporary home with Him for a thousand years. Our permanent home is the New Heaven and Earth (New Jerusalem) in which we will be there with Him forever and ever.

EXODUS 33 – SHOW ME YOUR GLORY

Exodus 33:18-33 (KJV)

¹⁸ And he said, I beseech thee, shew me thy Glory.

¹⁹ And He said, I will make all My Goodness pass before thee, and I will proclaim the Name of the Lord before thee; and will be gracious to whom I will be gracious, and will shew mercy on whom I will shew mercy.

²⁰ And He said, Thou canst not see My face: for there shall no man see Me, and live.

²¹ And the Lord said, Behold, there is a place by Me, and thou shalt stand upon a rock:

Exodus 33 – Show Me Your Glory

²² And it shall come to pass, while My Glory passeth by, that I will put thee in a cleft of the rock, and will cover thee with My hand while I pass by:

²³ And I will take away Mine hand, and thou shalt see My back parts: but My face shall not be seen.

Moses asked the Lord to show him His Glory and He did. This request is also revealed in the scriptures by the psalmist, David, in Psalm 24:7-10, which reads. *"Lift up your heads, O ye gates; and be ye lift up, ye everlasting doors; and the King of Glory shall come in. Who is this King of Glory? The LORD strong and mighty, the LORD mighty in battle. Lift up your heads, O ye gates; even lift them up, ye everlasting doors; and the King of Glory shall come in. Who is this King of Glory? The LORD of Hosts, He is the King of Glory. Selah."*

The Lord showed Moses the "soon-coming" promised Messiah, Jesus, the Word of God made flesh. The Apostle John tells us in John 1:1-3, 14 which says, *"In the beginning was the Word, and the Word was with God, and the Word was God. The Same was in the beginning with God. All things were made by Him; and without Him was not any thing made that was made... And the Word was made flesh, and dwelt among us, (and we beheld His Glory, the Glory as of the only begotten of the Father,) full of grace and truth."*

The book of Hebrews tells us that Jesus will come in the volume of the book written of Him. Hebrews 10:5-7 says, *"Wherefore when He cometh into the world, He saith, Sacrifice and offering Thou wouldest not, but a body hast Thou prepared Me: In burnt offerings and sacrifices for sin Thou hast had no pleasure. Then said I, Lo, I come (in the volume of the book it is written of Me,) to do Thy will, O God."*

The Lord God told Moses there is a place by Him. The place that the Lord was referring to is at the right hand of the Father where Jesus, the Word is seated. Hebrews 1:3 says, *"God, Who at sundry times and in divers manners spake in time past unto the fathers by the prophets, Hath in these last days spoken unto us by His Son, Whom He hath appointed Heir of all things, by Whom also He made the worlds; Who being the brightness of His Glory, and the express image of His Person, and upholding all things by the word of His Power, when He had by Himself purged our sins, sat down on the right hand of the Majesty on high."*

The Lord tells Moses to stand upon a rock. This Rock is Jesus. Deuteronomy 32:4 says, *"He is the Rock, His work is perfect: for all His ways are judgment: a God of Truth and without iniquity, just and right is He."* **The Apostle Peter tells us in 1st Peter 2:6-8,** *"Wherefore also it is contained in the scripture, Behold, I lay in Sion a Chief Corner Stone, elect, precious: and he that believeth on Him shall not be confounded. Unto you therefore which believe He is precious: but unto them which be disobedient, the Stone which the builders disallowed, the Same is made the head of the corner, and a Stone of*

Exodus 33 – Show Me Your Glory

Stumbling, and a Rock of Offence, even to them which stumble at the word, being disobedient: whereunto also they were appointed." The scripture also lets us know that in 1st Corinthians 3:11, *"For other foundation can no man lay than that is laid, which is Jesus Christ."*

The Lord continues to tells Moses that, *"it shall come to pass, while My Glory passeth by., that I will put thee in a cleft of the rock, and will cover thee with My hand while I pass by."* The Lord puts Moses in the cleft of the rock signifying that Jesus is the Rock that He placed Moses within. We know that when Jesus died on the cross, the Roman soldier pierced Him in the side creating a cleft for all believers, Jew and Gentile, to be redeemed and pardoned. John 19:31-37 says that *"The Jews therefore, because it was the preparation, that the bodies should not remain upon the cross on the Sabbath Day, (for that Sabbath Day was an High Day,) besought Pilate that their legs might be broken, and that they might be taken away. Then came the soldiers, and brake the legs of the first, and of the other which was crucified with Him. But when they came to Jesus, and saw that He was dead already, they brake not His legs: But one of the soldiers with a spear pierced His side, and forthwith came there out blood and water. And he that saw it bare record, and his record is true: and he knoweth that he saith true, that ye might believe. For these things were done, that the scripture should be fulfilled, A bone of Him shall not be broken. And again another scripture saith, They shall look on Him Whom they pierced."*

Exodus 33 – Show Me Your Glory

Now, we have been justified by Jesus' blood and finished works on the cross at Calvary. Ephesians 2:13-22 says, *"But now in Christ Jesus ye who sometimes were far off are made nigh by the blood of Christ. For He is our peace, Who hath made both one, and hath broken down the middle wall of partition between us; Having <u>abolished in His flesh the enmity</u>, even the law of commandments contained in ordinances; for to make in Himself of twain one new man, so making peace; And that He might reconcile both unto God in one body by the cross, having slain the enmity thereby: And came and preached peace to you which were afar off, and to them that were nigh. For through Him we both have access by one Spirit unto the Father. Now therefore ye are no more strangers and foreigners, but fellowcitizens with the saints, and of the household of God; And are built upon the foundation of the apostles and prophets, Jesus Christ Himself being the Chief Corner Stone; In Whom all the building fitly framed together groweth unto an holy temple in the Lord: In whom ye also are builded together for an habitation of God through the Spirit."*

Jesus is the Glory of the Father that came through forty-two generations in order to redeem all mankind from the grip of Satan. Jesus was wounded for our transgressions, bruised for our iniquities, the chastisement of our peace was upon Him, and with his stripes, we are healed (Isaiah 53:5). He destroyed all of the works of the devil which are sin and death through the veil (cleft) of His flesh. Through a new and better covenant, our sins have been forgiven. Without the shedding of His blood, there is no remission

Exodus 33 – Show Me Your Glory

(forgiveness) of sin. Jesus is the only Way to the Father for redemption. He is the Way, the Truth, and the Life and no man cometh to the Father, but by Him (John 14:6). Now we can say *"Blessed is the man whose sins are forgiven and the Lord will not impute iniquities."* Through His resurrection we have been justified as if we have never sinned (Romans 4:25). He died once and for all and there is no more offering for sin. Romans 8:33-39 says it best, *"Who shall lay any thing to the charge of God's elect? It is God that justifieth. Who is he that condemneth? It is Christ that died, yea rather, that is risen again, Who is even at the right hand of God, Who also maketh intercession for us. Who shall separate us from the love of Christ? shall tribulation, or distress, or persecution, or famine, or nakedness, or peril, or sword? As it is written, For Thy sake we are killed all the day long; we are accounted as sheep for the slaughter. Nay, in all these things we are more than conquerors through Him that loved us. For I am persuaded, that neither death, nor life, nor angels, nor principalities, nor powers, nor things present, nor things to come, nor height, nor depth, nor any other creature, shall be able to separate us from the love of God, which is in Christ Jesus our Lord."*

GENESIS 4 - THE PURPOSE OF CAIN AND ABEL'S OFFERINGS (BODY AND BLOOD OF JESUS)

Genesis 4:3-13 (KJV)

³ And in process of time it came to pass, that Cain brought of the fruit of the ground an offering unto the Lord.

⁴ And Abel, he also brought of the firstlings of his flock and of the fat thereof. And the Lord had respect unto Abel and to his offering:

⁵ But unto Cain and to his offering He had not respect. And Cain was very wroth, and his countenance fell.

⁶ And the Lord said unto Cain, Why art thou wroth? and why is thy countenance fallen?

Genesis 4 - The Purpose of Cain and Abel's Offerings
(Body and Blood of Jesus)

⁷ If thou doest well, shalt thou not be accepted? and if thou doest not well, sin lieth at the door. And unto thee shall be his desire, and thou shalt rule over him.

⁸ And Cain talked with Abel his brother: and it came to pass, when they were in the field, that Cain rose up against Abel his brother, and slew him.

⁹ And the Lord said unto Cain, Where is Abel thy brother? And he said, I know not: Am I my brother's keeper?

¹⁰ And He said, What hast thou done? the voice of thy brother's blood crieth unto Me from the ground.

¹¹ And now art thou cursed from the earth, which hath opened her mouth to receive thy brother's blood from thy hand;

¹² When thou tillest the ground, it shall not henceforth yield unto thee her strength; a fugitive and a vagabond shalt thou be in the earth.

¹³ And Cain said unto the Lord, My punishment is greater than I can bear.

Cain's offering was the most holy offering of all (the bread and body of our Lord). According to Leviticus chapter 2, the grain offering is a food offering of grain beaten into fine flour without yeast, mingled with oil, frankincense, and salt. It was presented by fire to the Lord. It is an aroma pleasing to the Lord. It is presented by fire to the Lord.

Genesis 4 - The Purpose of Cain and Abel's Offerings (Body and Blood of Jesus)

His offering was the meat or grain offering and is symbolic of Jesus' body, the True Bread that came down from heaven, without sin, and crucified. Just like the preparation of the grain offering, Jesus' body was beaten, broken, and anointed with oil (spikenard) prior to His crucifixion and burial to fulfill His Genesis 3:16 promise and His salt covenants with Abraham (Genesis 12:1-3, 15:7-21, 22:15-18).

The salt covenant is an undissolvable and eternal covenant initiated by God. Galatians 3:13-17 says, *"Christ hath redeemed us from the curse of the law, being made a curse for us: for it is written, Cursed is every one that hangeth on a tree: That the blessing of Abraham might come on the Gentiles through Jesus Christ; that we might receive the promise of the Spirit through faith. Brethren, I speak after the manner of men; Though it be but a man's covenant, yet if it be confirmed, <u>no man disannulleth, or addeth thereto</u>. Now to Abraham and His Seed were the <u>promises</u> made. He saith not, And to seeds, as of many; but as of One, And to thy Seed, which is Christ. And this I say, that the covenant, that was confirmed before of God in Christ, the law, which was four hundred and thirty years after, <u>cannot disannul</u>, that it should make the promise of none effect."*

Jesus' body being anointed with spikenard was fulfilled in Matthew 26:7-13 with a woman having an alabaster box of very precious ointment (spikenard) poured it on His head. *"Now when Jesus was in Bethany, in the house of Simon the leper, There came*

Genesis 4 - The Purpose of Cain and Abel's Offerings
(Body and Blood of Jesus)

unto Him a woman having an alabaster box of very precious ointment, and poured it on His head, as He sat at meat. But when His disciples saw it, they had indignation, saying, To what purpose is this waste? For this ointment might have been sold for much, and given to the poor. When Jesus understood it, He said unto them, Why trouble ye the woman? For she hath wrought a good work upon Me. For ye have the poor always with you; but Me ye have not always. For in that she hath poured this ointment on My body, she did it for My burial. Verily I say unto you, Wheresoever this gospel shall be preached in the whole world, there shall also this, that this woman hath done, be told for a memorial of her."

She poured the spikenard upon Him for His burial because He was to beaten with 39 stripes and crucified (offered up) on a Roman cross and buried in the heart of the earth only to rise three days later on the Feast of First Fruits. Christ fulfilled these offerings on Passover, the Feast of Unleavened Bread, and the Feast of First Fruits. He is our Passover Sacrificial Lamb without blemish (sinless) and our High Priest. Isaiah chapter 53:5 says, *"He was wounded for our transgressions and He was bruised for our iniquities and the chastisement of our peace was upon Him and with His stripes we are healed."*

Abel's offering was the burnt offering symbolizing the blood offering (wine) for the forgiveness of sin. The burnt offering, according to Leviticus chapter 1, is a burnt sacrifice, an offering made by fire, of a sweet

Genesis 4 - The Purpose of Cain and Abel's Offerings (Body and Blood of Jesus)

savor to the Lord. Both offerings are offered at the same time and are symbolic of Christ's crucifixion, death, worship (obedience to the Father) and the fulfillment of the Lord's covenant (the salt covenant).

These offerings also deal with our relationship with the Lord and with one another just like when we take the bread and wine at Communion (this do in remembrance of Me).

First Corinthians 11:23-33 reads, *"For I have received of the Lord that which also I delivered unto you, that the Lord Jesus the same night in which He was betrayed took bread: And when He had given thanks, He brake it, and said, Take, eat: this is My body, which is broken for you: this do in remembrance of Me. After the same manner also He took the cup, when He had supped, saying, this cup is the new testament in My blood: this do ye, as oft as ye drink it, in remembrance of Me. For as often as ye eat this bread, and drink this cup, ye do shew the <u>Lord's death</u> till He come. Wherefore whosoever shall eat this bread, and drink this cup of the Lord, unworthily, shall be guilty of the body and blood of the Lord. But let a man examine himself, and so let him eat of that bread, and drink of that cup. For he that eateth and drinketh unworthily, eateth and drinketh damnation to himself, not discerning the Lord's body. For this cause many are weak and sickly among you, and many sleep. For if we would judge ourselves, we should not be judged. But when we are judged, we are chastened of the Lord, that we should not be condemned with the world. Wherefore, My*

Genesis 4 - The Purpose of Cain and Abel's Offerings
(Body and Blood of Jesus)

brethren, when ye come together to eat, tarry one for another."

This event is called Communion and is one of the two ordinances the Lord gave to His church to do in remembrance of Him. The other ordinance is water baptism in which we are completely submerged into the water after the confession of faith signifying His death, burial, and resurrection (Matthew 28:19-20; Romans 6:3-11). First Corinthians 10:16 says, *"The cup of blessing which we bless, is it not the communion of the <u>blood</u> of Christ? The bread which we break, is it not the communion of the <u>body</u> of Christ?"*

In the same 11th chapter of 1st Corinthians, Paul is referring to the divisions and heresies (beliefs and opinions contrary to the apostle's doctrine and holy scriptures) among Christ's body of believers so that they which are approved (authentic or genuine) may be made manifest (revealed) among them. In today's terminology, we call these actions "power struggles". This is why when partaking of Communion we are told prior to receiving the elements (the bread and wine) to examine ourselves because he that eat and drink unworthily, eat and drink damnation to himself. To not discern the Lord's body (the spiritual body of Christ), is why many are weak and sickly among you and many sleep.

He continues in the 12th chapter of 1st Corinthians to elaborate more on the same subject. He proceeds to tell us that the spiritual body of Christ is one with many

Genesis 4 - The Purpose of Cain and Abel's Offerings
(Body and Blood of Jesus)

members and that by one Spirit are we all baptized into one body, whether we be Jews or Gentiles, whether we be bond or free; and have been all made to drink into one Spirit. He continues to say that God set the members, every one of them, in the body as it pleased Him. We all need each other and cannot say we have no need of one another. Those that appear feeble (weak), less honorable (unimportant), more honorable (important), are all necessary. God has divinely orchestrated the body of Christ in such a way that He bestows extra honor and attention to those parts that might seem less or of no importance. Therefore, we are not to let there be a schism in the body. However, each member should genuinely exercise the same care one for another. When one member suffers, we all suffer with them and when one member is honored, we all rejoice with them.

In Matthew chapter 5:23-25, Jesus said, *"Therefore if thou bring thy gift to the altar, and there rememberest that thy brother hath ought against thee; Leave there thy gift before the altar, and go thy way; first be reconciled to thy brother, and then come and offer thy gift. Agree with thine adversary quickly, whiles thou art in the way with him; lest at any time the adversary deliver thee to the judge, and the judge deliver thee to the officer, and thou be cast into prison."*

Therefore, let us not be as Cain, but genuinely love our brothers and sisters in Christ as Jesus has commanded us to love one another and be reconciled to God and one another. Romans 12:9-21 says, *"Let love

Genesis 4 - The Purpose of Cain and Abel's Offerings (Body and Blood of Jesus)

be without dissimulation (without hypocrisy). Abhor that which is evil; cleave to that which is good. Be kindly affectioned one to another with brotherly love; in honour preferring one another; Not slothful in business; fervent in spirit; serving the Lord; Rejoicing in hope; patient in tribulation; continuing instant in prayer; Distributing to the necessity of saints; given to hospitality. Bless them which persecute you: bless, and curse not. Rejoice with them that do rejoice, and weep with them that weep. Be of the same mind one toward another. Mind not high things, but condescend to men of low estate. Be not wise in your own conceits. Recompense to no man evil for evil. Provide things honest in the sight of all men. If it be possible, as much as lieth in you, live peaceably with all men. Dearly beloved, avenge not yourselves, but rather give place unto wrath: for it is written, Vengeance is mine; I will repay, saith the Lord. Therefore if thine enemy hunger, feed him; if he thirst, give him drink: for in so doing thou shalt heap coals of fire on his head. Be not overcome of evil, but overcome evil with good." The *"heap coals of fire on his head"* means the goodness of the Lord leads to repentance. And in Galatians 6:10, *"As we have therefore opportunity, let us do good unto all men, especially unto them who are of the household of faith."*

    I will end this chapter by quoting two witnesses or scriptures. Luke 11:17-18, *"But He, knowing their thoughts, said unto them, <u>Every kingdom</u> divided against itself is brought to desolation; and a house divided against a house falleth. If Satan also be divided against himself, how shall his kingdom stand? because ye say that I cast*

Genesis 4 - The Purpose of Cain and Abel's Offerings (Body and Blood of Jesus)

out devils through Beelzebub." And **1st Corinthians 1:10-13,** *"Now I beseech you, brethren, by the name of our Lord Jesus Christ, that ye all speak the same thing, and that there be no divisions among you; but that ye be perfectly <u>joined together in the same mind and in the same judgment</u> (**purpose**). For it hath been declared unto me of you, my brethren, by them which are of the house of Chloe, that there are contentions among you. Now this I say, that every one of you saith, I am of Paul; and I of Apollos; and I of Cephas; and I of Christ. <u>Is Christ divided</u>? was Paul crucified for you? or were ye baptized in the name of Paul?"* There is not one kingdom that can stand if it is divided. Yet, we have church splits, divorces, relationships dissolve (personal and business), friends separate, and families divides, etc. Here are a few examples found in Proverbs.

Proverbs 16:28

"A froward man soweth strife: and a whisperer separateth chief friends."

Proverbs 17:9

"He that covereth a transgression seeketh love; but he that repeateth a matter separateth very friends."

Proverbs 6:16-19

[16] These six things doth the Lord hate: yea, seven are an abomination unto Him:

[17] A proud look, a lying tongue, and hands that shed innocent blood,

Genesis 4 - The Purpose of Cain and Abel's Offerings
(Body and Blood of Jesus)

^{18} An heart that deviseth wicked imaginations, feet that be swift in running to mischief,

^{19} A false witness that speaketh lies, and he that soweth discord among brethren.

Therefore, let us be obedient, love one another, and do good to all men, especially to those of the household of faith (1st John 4:7-8; John 14:23-24; Galatians 6:10). Let us not love in word, neither in tongue; but in deed and in truth (1st John 3:18). After all, by love shall all men know that we are His disciples (John 13:35). This is not an impossible thing to do since God is Love and Love dwells within each believer. Therefore, we can produce fruits of love.

CHAPTER ONE

The Revelation of Jesus Christ which God gave to John to show His servants things which must shortly come to pass. He sent and signified it by His angel to His servant, John. John bears record of the Word of God, the testimony of Jesus Christ, and of all things that he saw. Blessed is he that reads, and they that hear the words of this prophecy and keeps those things which are written because the time is at hand.

John begins his letter to the seven churches which are in Asia. *"Grace be unto you, and peace, from Him which <u>is</u>, and which <u>was</u>, and which <u>is to come</u>; and from the seven Spirits which are before His throne; And from Jesus Christ, Who is the Faithful Witness, and the First Begotten of the dead, and the Prince of the kings of the earth. Unto Him that loved us, and washed us from our sins in His own blood, And hath made us kings and*

Chapter One

priests unto God and His Father; to Him be glory and dominion for ever and ever. Amen."

Then John lets us know that *"Behold, He cometh with clouds; and every eye shall see Him, and they also which pierced Him: and all kindreds of the earth shall wail because of Him. Even so, Amen."*

Jesus says to John, *"I am Alpha and Omega, the Beginning and the Ending, saith the Lord, which is, and which was, and which is to come, the Almighty."*

John authenticates the author of this letter by letting us know that *"I John, who is your brother and companion in tribulation (suffering - not the great tribulation) and in the kingdom and patience of Jesus Christ, was on the isle that is called Patmos for the word of God and for the testimony of Jesus Christ."* He lets us know that he was in the spirit on the Lord's Day (Sunday) and heard behind him a great voice as of a trumpet, *"Saying, I am Alpha and Omega, the First and the Last: and, What thou seest, write in a book, and send it unto the seven churches which are in Asia; unto Ephesus, and unto Smyrna, and unto Pergamos, and unto Thyatira, and unto Sardis, and unto Philadelphia, and unto Laodicea."* These were actual churches and are symbolic of the characteristics of the saints and their behavior in the church which is Christ's spiritual body. The church as a whole is one body. First Corinthians 12:12-14, *"For as the body is one, and hath many members, and all the members of that one body, being many, are one body: so also is Christ. For by one Spirit are we all baptized into one body, whether we be Jews or*

Chapter One

Gentiles, whether we be bond or free; and have been all made to drink into one Spirit. For the body is not one member, but many." Therefore, the current day church, as a whole, consists of more than just these seven churches (houses of worship) located in Asia. There are believers on all seven continents.

The Vision of the Son of Man

John turns to see the voice that spoke with Him and saw seven golden candlesticks. In the midst of the seven candlesticks, One, like the Son of Man, clothed with a garment down to the foot and a golden sash around His chest. His head and hair were white like wool and white as snow. His eyes were as a flame of fire. His feet were like fine brass (bronze) as if they were burned in a furnace. His voice was as the sound of many waters. He had in His right hand seven stars. Out of His mouth went a sharp two-edged sword. His countenance was as the sun shining in its strength. When John saw Him, John fell at His feet as dead. He laid His right hand upon John saying, *"Fear not; I am the First and the Last: I am He that liveth, and was dead; and, behold, I am alive for evermore, Amen; and have the keys of hell and of death. Write the things which thou <u>hast seen</u>, and the things which <u>are</u>, and the things which <u>shall be hereafter</u>."*

Jesus is also fulfilling the prophecy that He spoke to Peter concerning John in John 21:21-24 saying, *"Peter seeing Him saith to Jesus, Lord, and what shall this man (John) do? Jesus saith unto him, If I will that he tarry till*

Chapter One

I come, what is that to thee? follow thou Me. Then went this saying abroad among the brethren, that that disciple should not die: yet Jesus said not unto him, he shall not die; but, If I will that he tarry till I come, what is that to thee? This is the disciple which testifieth of these things, and wrote these things: and we know that his testimony is true." Therefore, He appears to John personally on the isle of Patmos and gives him the book of Revelation to write to the churches.

The Mystery of the Seven Stars and the Seven Golden Candlesticks.

Jesus, the Son of Man, tells John the mystery of the seven stars which John saw in Jesus' right hand and the seven golden candlesticks. The seven stars are the angels (pastors) of the seven churches and the seven candlesticks which John saw are the seven churches.

CHAPTER TWO

The Church Of Ephesus

To the angel of the church of Ephesus write the words of Jesus that holds the seven stars in His right hand and Who walks in the midst of the seven golden candlesticks. I know of your works, your labor, your perseverance, and how you cannot bear them which are evil. You have tried them which say they are apostles, and are not, and have found them liars. You have persevered and endured for My name's sake and have labored and have not grown weary.

Nevertheless, I have something against you because you have left your first love. Remember, therefore, from where you have fallen. Repent and do the first works or else I will come to you quickly and will remove your candlestick out of its place, except you repent. But this you have, you hate the deeds of the Nicolaitanes which I also hate. He that has an ear, let him hear what the Spirit says to the churches. To him that overcomes, I will give to eat of the Tree of Life which is in the midst of the Paradise (New Jerusalem) of God (Revelation 22:2-3).

The Church In Smyrna

To the angel of the church in Smyrna write the words of the First and the Last, Who was dead and is alive. I know your works, tribulation, and poverty (but, you are rich). I know of the blasphemy of them which say they are Jews and are not, but are the synagogue of Satan. Fear none of those things which you shall suffer. Behold, the devil will cast some of you into prison so that you may be tried. You will have tribulation for ten days. Be faithful to death and I will give you a crown of life. He that has an ear, let him hear what the Spirit says to the churches. He that overcomes will not be hurt of the second death (eternal damnation or lake of fire).

Smyrna is known as the persecuted church. It is the only church that will be raptured with the other churches and endure the great tribulation. The entire body of Christ will be raptured or caught up at the sound of the last (seventh) trumpet except for the 144,000 sealed Jewish believers. There are individuals who will be saved, after the rapture of the church, during the great tribulation period. These tribulation saints will not worship the Antichrist, his image, nor will they take the mark of the beast. Some of them will be persecuted and martyred for rejecting the Antichrist, his image, and his mark. The ten days of tribulation includes 2 days (2,000 years the current church age), 7 days (the week of Daniel which includes 3 ½ years for the great tribulation) and the Day of Atonement (the tenth day - Second Advent) (2nd Peter 3:8; Daniel 9:27; Hosea 6:1-3). These days corresponds with the Feast of Trumpets (current New Testament church age) being on the 1st day in the seventh month and the Day of Atonement occurring on the 10th day of the same seventh month (Leviticus 23:23-32). When I say church age, I am referring to the time period beginning from Jesus' earthly ministry, crucifixion, resurrection until his Second Advent or Physical Coming. What Jesus did at Calvary on Golgotha's Hill cannot be undone by anyone or anything ever. Jesus purchased the church with His Own blood once and for all and made salvation available to all men to whosoever will believe on Him (Hebrews 9, 9:24-28). After ten days, the Judgment Seat of Christ occurs on earth and then there will be a rest. Smyrna (those resurrected before and after the great tribulation) will receive crowns. At Christ Second Advent (Day of Atonement) there will be a rest ushering in the Millennial reign of Christ in which Satan will be chained in a bottomless pit during the entire Millennium (Revelation 20:1-3).

The Church In Pergamos

To the angel of the church in Pergamos write the words of He Who has the sharp double-edged sword. I know your works and where you dwell, even where Satan's seat (throne) is located. You hold fast to My name and have not denied My faith even in those days where Antipas was, My faithful martyr, who was slain among you where Satan dwells. But, I have a few things against you because you have those there that hold the doctrine of Balaam, who taught Balak to cast a stumbling block before the children of Israel to eat things sacrificed to idols and to commit fornication. Also, you have those that hold the doctrine of the Nicolaitanes, which thing I hate. Repent or else I will come to you quickly and will fight against them with the sword of My mouth. He that has an ear, let him hear what the Spirit says to the churches. To him that overcomes, I will give to eat of the hidden manna. I will also give him a white stone. And on the stone, a new name is written which no man knows except he that receives it.

The Church In Thyatira

To the angel of the church in Thyatira write the words of the Son of God Who have eyes like a flame of fire and feet like fine brass (bronze). I know your works of charity (love), service, faith, your patience (perseverance), and your works; and the last to be more than the first. I have a few things against you because you allow that woman Jezebel, who calls herself a prophetess, to teach and to seduce my servants to commit fornication and to eat things sacrificed to idols. I gave her time to repent of her fornication and she repented not. Behold, I will cast her into a bed and

Chapter Two

those who commit adultery with her into great tribulation except they repent of their deeds. I will kill her children with death then all the churches will know that I am He Who searches the minds and hearts. I will give to every one of you according to your works. But, I say to you and the rest in Thyatira and to as many as have not received this doctrine and who have not known the depths of Satan, as they speak. I will put upon you no other burden, but that which you have already. Hold fast until I come. To him that overcomes and keeps my works to the end, I will give power over the nations. He will rule those during the Millennium with a rod of iron. As the vessels of a potter, they will be broken to shivers: even as I received authority of My Father. I will give him the morning star. He that has an ear, let him hear what the Spirit say to the churches.

CHAPTER THREE

The Church In Sardis

To the angel of the church in Sardis write the words of He that have the seven Spirits of God and the seven stars. I know your works. You have a name (reputation) that you are alive and you are dead. Be watchful and strengthen the things which remain, which are ready to die: because I have found your works to be not perfect before God. Remember, therefore, how you have received and heard. Hold fast and repent. Therefore, if you will not watch, I will come upon you as a thief and you will not know the hour. You have a few people in Sardis who have not defiled their garments. They will walk with me clothed in white because they are worthy. He that overcomes will be clothed in white raiment. I will not blot his name out of the Book of Life, but I will confess his name before

Chapter Three

My Father and before His angels. He that has an ear, let him hear what the Spirit say to the churches.

The Church In Philadelphia

To the angel of the church in Philadelphia write the words of He that is Holy, He that is True, He that has the key of David, He that opens and no man shuts; and shuts and no man opens. I know your works. Behold, I have set before you an open door and no man can shut. You have a little strength and have kept My word and have not denied My name. Behold, I will make them of the synagogue of Satan, which say they are Jews, and are not, but do lie; behold, I will make them to come and worship before your feet and to know that I have loved you. Because you have kept the word of my patience, I also will keep you from the hour of temptation which shall come upon the entire world to try them that dwell upon the earth. Behold, I come quickly. Hold fast to that which you have so that no man takes your crown. To him that overcomes will I make a pillar in the temple of My God and he shall go no more out. I will write upon him the name of My God and the name of the city of My God, which is New Jerusalem, which comes down out of heaven from My God. I will write upon him My new name. He that hath an ear, let him hear what the Spirit say to the churches.

The Church Of The Laodiceans

To the angel of the church of the Laodiceans write the words of the Amen, the Faithful and True Witness,

Chapter Three

the Beginning of the creation of God. I know your works and that you are neither cold nor hot. I would prefer you were either cold or hot. Because you are lukewarm and neither cold nor hot, I will spit you out of my mouth. Because you say I am rich and increased with goods and have need of nothing; and know not that you are wretched, miserable, poor, blind, and naked. I counsel you to buy of Me gold tried in the fire so that you may be rich; and white raiment so that you may be clothed and the shame of your nakedness does not appear. Anoint your eyes with eye salve so that you may see. As many as I love, I rebuke and chasten: be zealous therefore, and repent. Behold, I stand at the door and knock. If any man hears My voice and opens the door, I will come into him and will sup with him and he with Me. To him that overcomes will I grant to sit with Me in My throne, even as I also overcame, and am set down with My Father in His throne. He that has an ear, let him hear what the Spirit say to the churches.

CHAPTER FOUR

Declaring The End From The Beginning

In chapters four and five, the Lord God is giving us John a glimpse into the Third Heaven, Paradise, during the Millennium, prior to the opening of the seven seals. John is viewing the <u>Tabernacle of God</u>, which is in the Third Heaven, in which Moses was told by God to pattern the earthly tabernacle (Exodus 25:9, 40). It is this tabernacle that Christ entered to sprinkle His blood. Hebrews 9:24 says, *"For Christ is not entered into the holy places made with hands, which are the figures of the true; but into heaven itself, now to appear in the presence of God for us."*

This vision is the predetermined plan of God written on a scroll before the foundation of the world. In Isaiah 46:9-10 God says, *"Remember the former things of old:*

Chapter Four

for I am God, and there is none else; I am God, and there is none like Me, declaring the end from the beginning, and from ancient times the things that are not yet done, saying, My counsel shall stand, and I will do all My pleasure: calling a ravenous bird from the east, the man that executeth My counsel from a far country: yea, I have spoken it, I will also bring it to pass; I have purposed it, I will also do it." In the mind of God, the Lamb of God was slain before the foundation of the world. First Corinthians 2:7-8 says, *"But we speak the wisdom of God in a mystery, even the hidden wisdom, which God ordained before the world unto our glory: Which none of the princes of this world knew: for had they known it, they would not have crucified the Lord of Glory."*

Other Scripture References:

1st Peter 1:19-21

[19] But with the precious blood of Christ, as of a lamb without blemish and without spot:

[20] Who verily was foreordained before the foundation of the world, but was manifest in these last times for you.

Acts 2:22-24

[22] Ye men of Israel, hear these words; Jesus of Nazareth, a Man approved of God among you by miracles and wonders and signs, which God did by Him in the midst of you, as ye yourselves also know:

[23] Him, being delivered by the determinate counsel and foreknowledge of God, ye have taken, and by wicked hands have crucified and slain:

Chapter Four

²⁴ Whom God hath raised up, having loosed the pains of death: because it was not possible that He should be holden of it.

<u>Hebrews 10:7</u>

⁷ Then said I, Lo, I come (in the volume of the book it is written of me,) to do thy will, O God.

The Heavenly Vision

In this chapter, a door was opened in heaven and the first voice which John heard as of a trumpet said, *"Come up hither, and I will shew thee things which must be hereafter."* John was caught up to the Third Heaven (Paradise) just like the man Paul mentions in 2nd Corinthians 12:1-5 which says, *"It is not expedient for me doubtless to glory. I will come to visions and revelations of the Lord. I knew a man in Christ above fourteen years ago, (whether in the body, I cannot tell; or whether out of the body, I cannot tell: God knoweth;) such an one caught up to the third heaven. And I knew such a man, (whether in the body, or out of the body, I cannot tell: God knoweth;) How that he was caught up into Paradise, and heard unspeakable words, which it is not lawful for a man to utter. Of such an one will I glory: yet of myself I will not glory, but in mine infirmities."* This man, just like John, was caught up into Paradise and heard unspeakable words which are not lawful for a man to utter. John was told not to write what was spoken by the seven thunders (Revelation 10:4).

Chapter Four

Chapter 4 is not the catching away of the saints or the rapture of the church as some would say. He is speaking solely to John. First Corinthians 15:51-52 says, *"Behold, I shew you a mystery; we shall not all sleep, but we shall all be changed, in a moment, in the twinkling of an eye, at the last trump: for the trumpet shall sound, and the dead shall be raised incorruptible, and we shall be changed."* When the catching away of the saints occurs, it will be in a moment in the twinkling of the eye as the scripture states. It will be faster than the time it takes to say "Come up hither (here)." We also know that this is not the catching away of the saints because, in Revelation 10:11, John is told by the angel that he (John) must prophesy again before many peoples, nations, tongues, and kings. When the catching away of the saints occurs, the saints will not return to earth until they come back with Jesus (The Word of God) in the air at His Second Advent (Physical Coming). This is also not the rapture of the church because if it was, then the Apostle John will still be here to be caught up or raptured together, at the same time, with the rest of the church. And we know that the Apostle John is already in heaven. Therefore, the rapture of the church or catching away of the saints does not occur here, but at the sound of the last (seventh) trumpet. The angel tells John in Revelation 10:6-7 that when the seventh angel sounds there should be time no longer and the mystery of God should be finished as He has declared to His servants the prophets. We do not know the day nor the hour when the seventh angel will sound his trumpet. But, we do

Chapter Four

know that after he does sound, the church is caught up or raptured at that time. Then, the great tribulation will occur because the time of God's wrath has come and we know how long that will last (Daniel 9:27; Matthew 24:14-22; Mark 13:14-20; Luke 21:20-22; Revelation 16:1).

John, in the Spirit, is allowed to see the One seated on a throne Who is God, the Father, in all of His Glory. He that sat on the throne looked like a jasper and sardius stone. He also sees a rainbow around the throne like an emerald. The scripture says in Psalm 84:11, *"For the Lord God is a Sun and Shield: the Lord will give grace and glory: no good thing will He withhold from them that walk uprightly."* And in Matthew 17:2 it says, *"And was transfigured before them: and His face did shine as the sun, and His raiment was white as the light."*

There is a rainbow around the throne. God, the Father, made a promise to Noah and every living creature of all flesh for future generations. God tells Noah that He will not destroy the earth and all flesh again by a flood. The rainbow in the clouds is a token sign of that covenant. God said in Genesis 9:16 that He will look upon the rainbow and remember the everlasting covenant between God and every living creature of all flesh that is upon the earth. The rainbow, in the third heaven, is also a reminder to Himself of the promise He made to Noah and all flesh. No matter which way He turns He sees the rainbow.

He also sees twenty-four elders round about the throne seated, clothed in white raiment, with crowns of

Chapter Four

gold on their heads praising God. John tells us that these are twenty-four elders. The golden crowns that the twenty-four elders are wearing let us know that they have already been to the Judgment Seat of Christ. We know that at Jesus' Second Advent, after the Great Tribulation, all of the saints of God, Jewish and Gentile believers, along with the nation of Israel at His coming will receive their crowns (rewards) at the same time (Matthew 16:27; Revelation 11:18, 22:12; 1st Peter 5:4). These twenty-four elders are figuratively representing the twenty-four sons of Aaron around the golden-crowned table of showbread or Bread of His Presence (1st Chronicles 24:1-19; Exodus 25:23-30; Leviticus 24:5-9). The twenty-four sons of Aaron were told to eat the bread in His Presence in The Holy Place or The Inner Court (Leviticus 24:9). In the model prayer, *"Give us this day our daily bread"* is what Jesus taught us to pray (Matthew 6:11; Luke 11:3). Our God supplies all of our need according to His riches in glory by Christ Jesus (Philippians 4:19). I believe these twenty-four elders who are crowned and seated around the throne of God are the twelve apostles and twelve sons of Jacob (Israel) representing the church fathers and the nation of Israel. Jesus our High Priest, promised the apostles (disciples) that they will sit on thrones in His kingdom (Matthew 19:28; Luke 22:29-30; Revelation 20:4). In the earthly tabernacles, there was no place for the priests to be seated (Hebrews 10:10-14). They are worshippers seated on thrones and crowned in Revelation chapters 4 and 5. In Revelation chapter 21, the names of the twelve tribes of Israel are written on the gates and the names of the twelve apostles of the Lamb are written on the twelve foundations in the New Heaven and New Earth.

Out of the throne proceeded lightnings, thunderings, and voices. There are seven lamps of fire burning before the throne, which are the seven Spirits of God or the Holy Spirit figuratively represented by the golden candlestick in the earthly tabernacle (Revelation 5:6; Isaiah 11:2-3). Seven is the number of perfection associated with the Godhead (James 1:17 & 25). Before the throne, there is a sea of glass like crystal. This is figurative of the laver made of brass (bronze) in the earthly tabernacle. Exodus 38:8 reads, *"And he made the laver of brass, and the foot of it of brass, of the lookingglasses of the women assembling, which assembled at the door of the tabernacle of the congregation."* The water in the laver is reflective causing a mirror appearance on the face of the water (Exodus 30:17-21, 38:8; 1st Corinthians 13:10, 12; James 1:22-27). It is the work of sanctification by the work of the Holy Spirit (Living Water) in the heart of a man (John 7:37-39; Philippians 2:12-16; John 16:7-15). Just like when we look into a mirror, we see ourselves as we are whether we are walking according to the will of God or whether we are walking according to the dictates of this world like the children of disobedience (Ephesians 2:1-10; Romans 6:12-18). This is the only item from the outer court that is in the third heaven. There is no need for the brazen altar in the third heaven because the Lamb of God was slain from the foundation of the world (Revelation 5:6). The brazen altar was located in the outer court.

In the midst of the throne and round about the throne were four beasts full of eyes before and behind. The first beast was like a lion, the second beast like a calf, and the third beast had a face as a man, and the fourth beast was like a flying eagle. Each of the four beasts had six wings and was full of eyes within. They rest neither day nor night saying, *"Holy, Holy, Holy, the L*ORD *God Almighty, which <u>Was</u>, and <u>Is</u>, and <u>Is To Come</u>."* These four beasts are seraphim (six-winged angels). Isaiah says in Isaiah 6:1-2, *"I saw the Lord, high and exalted, seated on a throne; and the train of His robe filled the temple. Above Him were seraphim, each with six wings: With two wings they covered their faces, with two they covered their feet, and with two they were flying. And they were calling to one another: "Holy, holy, holy is the L*ORD *Almighty; the whole earth is full of His Glory."*

Just like the rainbow, God is reminding Himself of His atoning blood covenant (promise) He made to all mankind via the gospel. No matter which way He turns He sees the gospel of grace. Some commentaries say that these four beasts represent the four different themes from which the four gospels are written. The lion (Matthew – Jesus, our King), calf or ox (Mark – Jesus, our Servant/Minister), face as a man (Luke – Jesus, the Son of Man), and a flying eagle (John – Jesus, the Son of God - I AM). Each gospel writer is telling the same gospel message of Christ from a different personage. The seraph told Isaiah in Isaiah 6:7, *"Your guilt is taken away and your sin atoned for."* Their message is the same message as the gospel of grace or the good news. These beasts give glory, honor, and thanks to Him that sit on the throne, Who lives forever and ever.

The twenty-four elders fall down before Him seated on the throne and worship Him that lives forever and ever. These elders cast their crowns before the throne, saying, *"Thou art worthy, O Lord, to receive glory and honor and power: for Thou hast created all things, and for Thy pleasure they are and were created."*

CHAPTER FIVE

The Heavenly Vision Continues

The vision continues with John seeing in the right hand of God, the Father, the One Who sits on the throne, a book was written inside and on the back side sealed with seven seals. Then John sees a strong angel proclaiming with a loud voice, *"Who is worthy to open the book, and to loose the seals thereof?"* No man in heaven, in the earth, or under the earth, was able to open the book, or to look there upon. John wept much because there was no man found worthy in heaven, in the earth, or under the earth who was able to open and to read the book or to look upon. One of the elders said to John, *"Weep not: behold, the Lion of the tribe of Judah, the Root of David, hath prevailed to open the*

Chapter Five

book, and to loose the seven seals thereof." **John beheld, and, lo, in the midst of the throne and of the four beasts, and in the midst of the elders, stood a Lamb as it had been slain, having seven horns and seven eyes, which are the seven Spirits of God, sent forth into all the earth (Isaiah 11:2). He came and took the book out of the right hand of Him that sits upon the throne. When He had taken the book, the four beasts and twenty-four elders fell down before the Lamb, having every one of them harps and golden vials full of odors, which are the prayers of saints. They sang a new song saying,** *"Thou art worthy to take the book, and to open the seals thereof: for Thou wast slain, and hast redeemed us to God by Thy blood out of every kindred, and tongue, and people, and nation; And hast made us unto our God kings and priests: and we shall reign on the earth."* **Notice that the twenty-four elders said** *"we shall reign on the earth"* **lets us know that this is a future prophecy. They are crowned. These elders will not receive crowns until they have been to the Judgment Seat of Christ which occurs at Christ's Second Advent.**

John beheld and heard the voice of many angels round about the throne and the beasts and the elders: and the number of them was ten thousand times ten thousand, and thousands of thousands; saying with a loud voice, *"Worthy is the Lamb that was slain to receive power, riches, wisdom, strength, honour, glory, and blessing."* **Every creature which is in heaven, on the earth, under the earth, in the sea, and all that is in them John heard saying,** *"Blessing, and honour, and glory,*

Chapter Five

and power, be unto Him that sitteth upon the throne, and unto the Lamb for ever and ever." The four beasts said, *"Amen."* The twenty-four elders fell down and worshipped Him that lives forever and ever. Again, this worship experience is a glimpse or preview into the third heaven during the Millennium because every creature is worshipping the Lord including those in hell and in the sea. There is no sea or hell in the New Heaven and the New Earth (New Jerusalem).

We see that no one was able to take the book and to open the seals because there is none worthy, but Christ, the Lamb of God. In Revelation 13:8, the scripture tells us that The Lamb of God was slain before the foundation of the world. I believe this book to be the entire prophetic vision or knowledge of all things to occur in the earth. This book contains Revelation's seven seals, seven trumpets, and seven vial judgments. In John 5:22-30, the Father has given all judgements (21) to the Son. Only God, the Father, knows the dates of certain events to occur. Matthew 24:34-36 says, *"Verily I say unto you, This generation shall not pass, till all these things be fulfilled. Heaven and earth shall pass away, but My words shall not pass away. But of that day and hour knoweth no man, no, not the angels of heaven, but My Father only."*

In Daniel, the 10th chapter, the angel, Gabriel, informs Daniel that there is a book of truth. He proceeds to tell him what is written in the Book of Truth. In Daniel 10: 20-21, *"Then said he, Knowest thou wherefore I come unto thee? and now will I return to*

Chapter Five

fight with the prince of Persia: and when I am gone forth, lo, the prince of Grecia shall come. But I will shew thee that which is noted in the scripture of truth: and there is none that holdeth with me in these things, but Michael your prince."

It is clearly evident that the angel knows of future events to come. In the chapters 11 and 12 of Daniel, he informs Daniel of future and end-time events. Some of these events have occurred and some will occur at the end-time exactly as written and prophesied. Each event will be fulfilled in their set time. He tells Daniel to shut up the words and seal the book until the time of the end. In Revelation 22:10, the angel tells the apostle John to seal not the sayings of the prophecy of this book because the time is at hand. *Revelation 22:6-10, "And he said unto me, these sayings are Faithful and True: and the Lord God of the holy prophets sent His angel to shew unto His servants the things which must shortly be done. Behold, I come quickly: blessed is he that keepeth the sayings of the prophecy of this book. And I John saw these things, and heard them. And when I had heard and seen, I fell down to worship before the feet of the angel which shewed me these things. Then saith he unto me, See thou do it not: for I am thy fellowservant, and of thy brethren the prophets, and of them which keep the sayings of this book: worship God. And he saith unto me, Seal not the sayings of the prophecy of this book: for the time is at hand."*

CHAPTER SIX

The Seven Seals (Was)

According to The New Strong's Exhaustive Concordance of the Bible, a seal is an instrument used to authenticate ownership. It signifies ownership so that only the owner can open and reveal its contents to whomever he or she pleases. In this case, the owner is God, the Father.

It is used figuratively of hidden things for protection until a certain time or use. For example, believers are sealed until the redemption of the purchased possession to the praise of His glory (Ephesians 1:14). The 144,000 Jewish believers are sealed prior to the great tribulation (Revelation 7:2-8). Even, the stars were sealed in Job

Chapter Six

9:7. I personally believe that the stars were sealed prior to the Genesis 1:2.

These seven seals are the unveiling of events that were previously sealed. In the 9th chapter of Daniel, the angel, Gabriel, tells Daniel that he will show him that which is written in the scripture of truth. And in the 12th chapter, he continues to tell Daniel of future events such as the time of Jacob's trouble and their deliverance. He informs Daniel that many who are sleep in the dust of the earth shall awake, some to everlasting life, and some to shame and everlasting contempt. He then tells Daniel to shut up the words and seal the book for the words are closed up and sealed until the time of the end.

These seven seals which are opened by the Lamb of God cover events that occur from Genesis to Revelation in order to give the church/believer a better understanding of God's love, grace, and mercies. After all, it is because of the Lord's mercies that we are not consumed (Lamentations 3:22).

The first four seals released include God's judgments (punishments) in the earth and they occurred in the book of Genesis at the fall of man (Adam) in the Garden of Eden. In Ezekiel chapter 14:21 which reads, *"For thus saith the Lord God; How much more when I send My four sore judgments upon Jerusalem, the sword, and the famine, and the noisome beast, and the pestilence, to cut off from it man and beast?"*

Chapter Six

Zechariah 6:1-5 says, *"And I turned, and lifted up mine eyes, and looked, and, behold, there came four chariots out from between two mountains; and the mountains were mountains of brass. In the first chariot were red horses; and in the second chariot black horses; And in the third chariot white horses; and in the fourth chariot grisled and bay horses. Then I answered and said unto the angel that talked with me, What are these, my lord? And the angel answered and said unto me, These are the four spirits of the heavens, which go forth from standing before the Lord of all the earth."*

These spirits of the heavens are angels who go forth from the Lord of all the earth and report to the Lord just like those in the book of Job. In Job 1:6-7, *"Now there was a day when the sons of God came to present themselves before the Lord, and Satan came also among them. And the Lord said unto Satan, Whence comest thou? Then Satan answered the Lord, and said, From going to and fro in the earth, and from walking up and down in it."* **And in Job 2:1-2,** *"Again there was a day when the sons of God came to present themselves before the Lord, and Satan came also among them to present himself before the Lord. And the Lord said unto Satan, From whence comest thou? And Satan answered the Lord, and said, From going to and fro in the earth, and from walking up and down in it."* **These sons of God are angels.**

1st Seal – Satan (Rider on White Horse)

Chapter Six

The Lamb of God opened the first seal and one of the four beasts said, *"Come and see."* The rider on the white horse is Lucifer, also known as Satan, the devil, the dragon, and the serpent. He hates all of mankind. First Peter 5:8 says, *"Be sober, be vigilant; because your adversary the devil, as a roaring lion, walketh about, seeking whom he may devour."* He wanted to be like the Most High and was cast down (Isaiah 14). The bible tells us that the thief (Satan) comes to steal, kill, and destroy (John 10:10). Jesus said that the world hates us (His disciples) because it hated Him first and because He testifies that their works are evil (John 15:18-19; Matthew 10:22; John 7:7).

Even though, we are created in God's image and likeness. We are not the Supreme and Sovereign God. God alone, the Godhead, is only Omnipotent, Omnipresent, Omniscient, and They are One. Satan opposes Christ, Christ teachings, Christ followers, and all unbelievers, thus operating in the spirit of the antichrist. He is a created spirit being. Satan, that old dragon, is pure evil (Isaiah 41). He is not equal in power with our Lord. He is a created being, not the Creator. He is a fallen angel with delegated power and is subject to Almighty God, Jesus, the Holy Spirit, and the name of Jesus.

Some believe this rider to be the Antichrist, the man of sin or lawlessness one, mentioned in the book of Revelation the chapter 13 who is also known as the first beast, but he is not. It is clear that this rider is Satan. Satan was given this authority (power) because of

Chapter Six

Adam's sin and disobedience. This is why Jesus did not correct nor rebuke Satan when he said in Luke 4:6 that *"All this power will I give thee, and the glory of them: for that is delivered unto me; and to whomsoever I will I give it."* Satan is called the prince of this world (John 12:31; 14:30). He will later give power to the Antichrist or the man of sin and the false prophet.

Satan was in the Garden of Eden from the very beginning (Ezekiel 28:13). The Lord God had commanded the man in Genesis 2:16-17 saying, *"Of every tree of the garden thou mayest freely eat: But of the tree of the knowledge of good and evil, thou shalt not eat of it: for in the day that thou eatest thereof thou shalt surely die."* Satan deceived Eve to eat the forbidden fruit from the tree of the knowledge of good and evil that was in the midst of the garden. Once, she ate the fruit from the forbidden tree and saw that she did not die, as the serpent had told her, she gave the forbidden fruit to Adam, her husband, and he did eat. The scripture states in 1st Timothy 2:13-14 that the woman was deceived and the man was not. It was not the woman's transgression that caused sin to enter into the world, but Adam's. As a result of Adam's fall, the Lord told him that *"dust thou art and unto dust shalt thou return."* The Lord told Satan (the serpent) that *"dust shalt thou eat all the days of thy life."* Since man is dust, then he definitely will be trying to devour man until Christ Second Advent.

When Adam fell, sin entered into the world and death by sin. The scripture states that in Adam all die (1st Corinthians 15:22). We were all in Adam's loins at the time of his fall. In Hebrews, Levi paid tithes through Abraham even though, he was in Abraham's loins (Hebrews 7:9). Eve was initially in Adam body and was surgically taken out of Adam's side by God (Genesis 2:21-23). Everything under Adam's dominion fell when he fell and became subject to sin and death (Romans 5:12, 8:19-23). Adam and Eve were now condemned, afraid, ashamed, and naked. They were never intended to die physically or to be spiritually separated from God but to live forever and ever in fellowship with God. According to Romans chapter 5 verse 12, death, physical and spiritual, was passed to all men. All have sinned and all are made sinners in Adam. Satan had conquered by causing the man to be spiritually separated from God. Because of Adam's fall, the man began to die physically and our bodies became corruptible (1st Corinthian 15:54).

The scripture refers to the unbelievers as children of disobedience. Satan, the devil, had the power over death until Jesus, the Christ, defeated him by Jesus' death on the cross and resurrection from the grave. Jesus paid our sin debt in full by giving His Life in exchange for ours and with the shedding of His blood, on a Roman's cross, there is forgiveness of sin. Jesus satisfied the wrath of God once and for all for every man that believes on Him Who was crucified and rose from the grave.

2nd Seal – Sword (War)

Chapter Six

The Lamb of God opened the second seal and the second beast said, *"Come and see."* **The rider on the red horse represents the sword (war) sent from God, the Father. Ezekiel chapter 14:13-21 says,** *"Son of man, when the land sinneth against Me by trespassing grievously, then will I stretch out Mine hand upon it, and will break the staff of the bread thereof, and will send famine upon it, and will cut off man and beast from it: Though these three men, Noah, Daniel, and Job, were in it, they should deliver but their own souls by their righteousness, saith the Lord God. If I cause noisome beasts to pass through the land, and they spoil it, so that it be desolate, that no man may pass through because of the beasts: Though these three men were in it, as I live, saith the Lord God, they shall deliver neither sons nor daughters; they only shall be delivered, but the land shall be desolate.* <u>*Or if I bring a sword upon that land, and say, Sword, go through the land; so that I cut off man and beast from it*</u>*: Though these three men were in it, as I live, saith the Lord God, they shall deliver neither sons nor daughters, but they only shall be delivered themselves. Or if I send a pestilence into that land, and pour out My fury upon it in blood, to cut off from it man and beast: Though Noah, Daniel, and Job were in it, as I live, saith the Lord God, they shall deliver neither son nor daughter; they shall but deliver their own souls by their righteousness. For thus saith the Lord God; How much more when I send* <u>*My four sore judgments*</u> *upon Jerusalem,* <u>*the sword, and the famine, and the noisome beast, and the pestilence*</u>*, to cut off from it man and beast?"* **Because of the fall of man, peace was taken**

Chapter Six

from the earth so that they should kill one another. The scripture notes that there was given to the red horse rider a great sword. As a result of this great sword, a spiritual war begins. Ephesians 6:12 says, *"For we wrestle not against flesh and blood, but against principalities, against powers, against the rulers of the darkness of this world, against spiritual wickedness in high places."* Satan has been warring against mankind since he tempted Eve and she led Adam to sin in the Garden of Eden. He even caused one of Adam's children to kill the other one.

We read in Genesis chapter 4 that Eve has given birth to two children, Cain and Abel. Cain was a tiller of the ground and Abel was a keeper of sheep. There came a day when each of them is bringing their offerings before the Lord God. Cain brought an offering to the Lord from the fruit of the ground (grain/meat offering) and Abel brought an offering of the firstlings of his flock and of the fat thereof (burnt offering). The Lord had respect for Abel's offering. But to Cain's offering, He had not respect. Cain became very wroth (angry) and his countenance fell because his offering was not accepted and his brother's offering was accepted. First John 3:12 tells us to be, *"Not as Cain, who was of that wicked one, and slew his brother. And wherefore slew he him? Because his own works were evil, and his brother's righteous."*

Cain had sin in his heart that led him to murder his brother Abel. According to Galatians 5:19-21, *"Now the works of the flesh are manifest, which are these;*

Chapter Six

Adultery, fornication, uncleanness, lasciviousness, idolatry, witchcraft, hatred, variance, emulations, wrath, strife, seditions, heresies, envyings, murders, drunkenness, revellings, and such like: of the which I tell you before, as I have also told you in time past, that they which do such things shall not inherit the kingdom of God." The scripture says that God looks on the heart and not as a man who looks on the outward appearance (1st Samuel 16:7). Mark 7:21-22 says, *"For from within, out of the heart of men, proceed evil thoughts, adulteries, fornications, murders, thefts, covetousness, wickedness, deceit, lasciviousness, an evil eye, blasphemy, pride, foolishness: All these evil things come from within, and defile the man."* In Genesis 4:7, the Lord told Cain *"If thou doest well, shalt thou not be accepted? and if thou doest not well, sin lieth at the door. And unto thee shall be his desire, and thou shalt rule over him."* He was telling Cain that sin's desires to master him, but he can rule over sin. Because he did not master sin, it deceived and slew himself as well (Romans 7:8-11).

Cain did not take those evil thoughts into captivity against his brother and bring them into the obedience of Christ. Second Corinthians 10:3-5 says, *"For though we walk in the flesh, we do not war after the flesh: (For the weapons of our warfare are not carnal, but mighty through God to the pulling down of strong holds;) Casting down imaginations, and every high thing that exalteth itself against the knowledge of God, and bringing into captivity every thought to the obedience of Christ."* Paul tells us in Ephesian 6:11-12 that we are to *"Put on the whole armour of God, that ye may be able to stand against the wiles of the devil. For we wrestle not against flesh and blood, but against principalities, against powers, against the rulers of the darkness of this world, against spiritual wickedness in high places."*

Adam and Eve have just experienced one consequence of disobedience, spiritual and physical death. Cain's wrath was taken out on Abel and now Abel is dead and Cain is a fugitive and a vagabond in the earth. For more information about Cain and Abel's offering see the chapter called *Genesis 4 - The Purpose of Cain and Abel's Offerings (Body and Blood of Jesus)*.

The man has become to know good and evil because Adam and Eve ate from the tree of the knowledge of good and evil. There is now an inward struggle (sword or war) within all mankind. Romans 7:21-25 says it best, *"I find then a law, that, when I would do good, evil is present with me. For I delight in the law of God after the inward man: but I see another law in my members, warring against the law of my mind, and bringing me into captivity to the law of sin which is in my members. O wretched man that I am! who shall deliver me from the body of this death? I thank God through Jesus Christ our Lord. So then with the mind I myself serve the law of God; but with the flesh the law of sin."* It is with the mind that we serve the Lord. The scripture tells us in 2nd Corinthians 10:3-5, *"For though we walk in the flesh, we do not war after the flesh: (For the weapons of our warfare are not carnal, but mighty through God to the pulling down of strong holds;) Casting down imaginations, and every high thing that exalteth itself*

Chapter Six

against the knowledge of God, and bringing into captivity every thought to the obedience of Christ." That is why all sin originates in the mind (our thought processes) and cause us to struggle with knowing good and evil, obedience and disobedience. Remember, Adam and Eve ate from the tree of the knowledge of good and evil. Paul said in Romans 7:21 that whenever he wanted to do good, evil was present. Now, that the believer is a new man and not carnally minded, the Holy Spirit helps us. In Philippians 2:12-13, *"Wherefore, my beloved, as ye have always obeyed, not as in my presence only, but now much more in my absence, work out your own salvation with fear and trembling. For it is God which worketh in you both to will and to do of His good pleasure."* Since the cross, there are three types of persons in the earth. They are the natural man, the carnal man, and the spiritual man.

The natural man is a sinner or an unbeliever and is fleshy. To be fleshy is to walk by their sinful nature or six senses and desires of the flesh. We know that the six senses are taste, touch, smell, sight, and touch (1st Corinthians 2:14; 6:9-11; Ephesians 4:22; Galatians 5:19-21). This man must be born again (John 3:1-7).

The carnal man is a believer with an unrenewed mind and still fleshy in the mind (his soul) and not in the heart (his spirit) which makes him to be in enmity, deep hatred or hostile, toward God (Romans 7:14-25, 8:5-8; 1st Corinthians 3:1-3; Galatians 5:16-17). Notice, that their enmity is toward God and not God's enmity toward them. God accepted Christ's blood sacrifice and made the believer accepted in the Beloved and blameless with a new heart or spirit (Ephesians 1:3-6; Colossians 1:22-23). Once and for all, Jesus satisfied the wrath of God because the chastisement of our peace was upon Christ. We are at peace with God (Romans 4:24-25; 5:1). There is still an inward struggle, especially for the carnal believer.

The spiritual man has a new heart or new nature, the new man, whose mind is renewed day by day and walk in the newness of spirit or life which is led by the Holy Spirit (Romans 7:6, 8:1-2, 13-17, 12:2; 1st Corinthians 2:9-13; Ephesians 4:23-24).

Therefore, let us not be as Cain, the wicked one, who slew his brother because his own works were evil, and his brother's righteous (1st John 3:12). Let us watch and pray that we enter not into temptation because the spirit indeed is willing, but the flesh is weak (Matthew 26:41). Jude 1:24 tells us that *"Now unto Him that is able to keep you from falling, and to present you faultless before the Presence of His Glory with exceeding joy."*

Another example of the effects of the sword is when David sinned with Bathsheba and had Uriah killed. The book of Samuel gives us a good understanding in 2nd Samuel 12:9-12 by saying, *"Wherefore hast thou despised the commandment of the Lord, to do evil in His sight? thou hast killed Uriah the Hittite with the sword, and hast taken his wife to be thy wife, and hast slain him with the sword of the children of Ammon. Now therefore the sword shall never depart from thine house; because thou hast despised Me, and hast taken the wife of Uriah the Hittite to be thy wife. Thus saith the Lord, Behold, I will raise up evil against thee out of thine own house, and I will take thy wives before thine eyes, and give them unto thy neighbour, and he shall lie with thy wives in the sight of this sun. For thou didst it secretly: but I will do this thing before all Israel, and before the sun."* Because of David's sin, the sword never left his household. The baby he had with Bathsheba dies as an infant. David's sons slay one another. Absalom had Amnon slain (2nd Samuel 13). Solomon had Adonijah slain because he was trying to take the kingdom from Solomon (1st Kings Chapters 1 and 2). Absalom rises up against David, his father, and temporarily takes the kingdom (2nd Samuel Chapters 15-19). Absalom sleeps with his father's concubines in sight of all in Israel (2nd Samuel 16:20-22).

Again, Jesus satisfied the wrath of God for all believers. Isaiah 53:5 says, *"But He was wounded for our transgressions, He was bruised for our iniquities: the chastisement of our peace was upon Him; and with His stripes we are healed."* Therefore, the believers will be spared from the great wrath to come which is the great tribulation or the seven vial judgments. First Thessalonians 1:10 says, *"And to wait for His Son from heaven, whom He raised from the dead, even Jesus, which delivered us from the wrath to come."* Christ has delivered us from the body of sin and death (Romans 7:23-24).

When a person confesses and accepts Christ as their personal Lord and Savior, they are saved and have power over sin (Romans 10:9-10). Romans 6:12-14 tells

Chapter Six

us to, *"Let not sin therefore reign in your mortal body, that ye should obey it in the lusts thereof. Neither yield ye your members as instruments of unrighteousness unto sin: but yield yourselves unto God, as those that are alive from the dead, and your members as instruments of righteousness unto God. For sin shall not have dominion over you: for ye are not under the law, but under grace."* In the same 6th chapter of Romans verses 1 and 2 states that *"What shall we say then? Shall we continue in sin, that grace may abound? God forbid. How shall we, that are dead to sin, live any longer therein?"* First John 3:4-10, *"Whosoever committeth sin transgresseth also the law: for sin is the transgression of the law. And ye know that He was manifested to take away our sins; and in Him is no sin. Whosoever abideth in Him sinneth not: whosoever sinneth hath not seen Him, neither known Him. Little children, let no man deceive you: he that doeth righteousness is righteous, even as he is righteous. He that committeth sin is of the devil; for the devil sinneth from the beginning. For this purpose the Son of God was manifested, that He might destroy the works of the devil. Whosoever is born of God doth not commit sin; for his seed remaineth in him: and he cannot sin, because he is born of God. In this the children of God are manifest, and the children of the devil: whosoever doeth not righteousness is not of God, neither he that loveth not his brother."* First John 5:18 tells us that *"We know that whosoever is born of God sinneth not; but he that is begotten of God keepeth himself, and that wicked one toucheth him not."*

Chapter Six

3rd Seal – Famine (Hunger)

The Lamb of God opened the third seal and the third beast said, *"Come and see."* The rider on the black horse with a pair of balances in his hand represents the famine (scarcity or hunger) sent from God, the Father. John hears a voice in the middle of the four living creatures say, *"A measure of wheat for a penny, and three measures of barley for a penny; and see thou hurt not the oil and the wine."* Proverbs 16:11 says, *"A just (honest) weight and balance are the Lord's: all the weights of the bag are His work (doings)."* God has judged or weighed the scales of man's (Adam and Eve) heart and obedience and found that they have fallen short of the glory of God (Romans 3:23, 5:15-19, 6:23). When Adam fell, everything (all creation) that he had dominion over fell to Satan, sin, and death. Even a newborn baby is born a sinner (Psalm 51:5). Adam's kingdom was taken into captivity by Satan just like when one king takes dominion over another king in war (Genesis 14:1-4). The defeated king (man) becomes subservient to the superior king (Satan, sin, and death) (Romans 7:14-25). Therefore, God expelled them from the Garden of Eden because they gave their authority to Satan when they ate from the tree of the knowledge of good and evil (Genesis 3:23-24; Romans 7:21). Satan is the god of this world. The devil boasts of his kingdom in a conversation with Jesus. Luke 4:5-6 reads, *"And the devil, taking Him up into an high mountain, shewed unto Him all the kingdoms of the world in a moment of time. And the devil said unto Him, All this power will I give Thee, and the glory of them: for that is delivered unto me; and to whomsoever I will I give it."* They are now sinners because they missed the mark and fell because of their disobedience. God also judged Satan and determined that Satan's kingdom is numbered and finished. He only has a short time. God said that the seed of the woman, Jesus, the Christ (Messiah), shall bruise Satan's head and Satan shall bruise Jesus' heel. This is very similar to Belshazzar's kingdom in Daniel chapter 5 being numbered by God and finished. God weighed Belshazzar heart or character in the balances and he was found wanting (fell short of God's standard). Daniel told Belshazzar that he should have learned from Nebuchadnezzar's fall and restoration. Belshazzar's kingdom was divided and given to the Medes and Persians in the same night.

God sends famine as a type of punishment. In Ezekiel 14:13, God states that *"when the inhabitants of the land sins (transgresses) against Him grievously, He will stretch out His hand upon it, and will break the staff of the bread (food supply) and will send famine upon it, and will cut off man and beast from it."*

Adam experienced a famine, a punishment of God, as a result of his disobedience. He went from the abundance of God's blessing, the Garden of Eden that the Lord God had planted, to being driven out of the Garden of Eden to till the ground from which he was taken (Genesis 2:8, 3:23-24). In other words, he was expelled from the garden of Eden and had to plant his own garden and provide food for him and his family.

Chapter Six

God said in Genesis 3:17-19, *"And unto Adam he said, Because thou hast hearkened unto the voice of thy wife, and hast eaten of the tree, of which I commanded thee, saying, Thou shalt not eat of it: <u>cursed is the ground</u> for thy sake; in sorrow shalt thou eat of it all the days of thy life; <u>Thorns also and thistles shall it bring forth to thee</u>; and thou shalt eat the herb of the field; In the sweat of thy face shalt thou eat bread, till thou return unto the ground; for out of it wast thou taken: for dust thou art, and unto dust shalt thou return."* **The ground was cursed because of Adam's fall and thorns and thistles it brought forth. Everything (all creation) that Adam had dominion over was subjected to the fall (Romans 8:19-23). Genesis 1:26 tells us of everything that man has dominion over when it says,** *"And God said, Let us make man in our image, after our likeness: and let them have dominion over the fish of the sea, and over the fowl of the air, and over the cattle, and <u>over all the earth</u>, and over every creeping thing that creepeth upon the earth."*

Therefore, the scripture states that the ground was cursed and in sorrow (toil) shall they eat the fruit of the earth all the days of their life. Thorns and thistles the earth will bring forth and by the sweat of the face shall they eat bread until they return to the ground (die). Adam and all mankind, before the flood, labored hard by the sweat of the face in order to cultivate and care for the earth. Their farming experience was not like it was in the Garden of Eden where the ground did not produce thorns and thistles. The ground would not yield itself to the man with ease, therefore creating much labor and resistance possibly producing a smaller

Chapter Six

harvest. According to the scripture, mankind was only eating herbs and bread prior to the Genesis chapter 9 (Genesis 1:29, 3:19, 9:3).

This punishment must have been very severe because God told Noah that He will not again curse the ground any more for man's sake. In Genesis 8:21, *"...the Lord said in His heart, I will not again curse the ground any more for man's sake; for the imagination of man's heart is evil from his youth; neither will I again smite any more every thing living, as I have done."* The entire earth (dry land) went through a physical water baptism known as the flood of Noah. In Genesis 6:17, God said, *"And, behold, I, even I, do bring a flood of waters upon the earth, to destroy all flesh, wherein is the breath of life, from under heaven; and every thing that is in the earth shall die."* Everyone and everything living with breath in their body died except Noah and his family, the only eight souls that were saved. In Genesis chapter 9, God blessed Noah and his sons again and told them to be fruitful, multiply, and replenish the earth. They were told that every moving thing that lives shall be meat (food) for them even as the vegetation that God had previously given them to eat. They are to bring forth abundantly in the earth and multiply (Genesis 9:1, 3, and 7).

Cain experienced this famine type of punishment as a result of murdering his brother, Abel. The Lord God told Cain to deal with his sin issue in his heart and that sin crouches at the door. Cain did not deal with the sin in his heart and slew his righteous brother (representing the oil and wine). The scripture says there came a day when they were in the field that Cain rose up against his brother Abel and slew him. The scripture goes on to say in Genesis 4:9-13, *"And the Lord said unto Cain, Where is Abel thy brother? And he said, I know not: Am I my brother's keeper? And He said, What hast thou done? the voice of thy brother's blood crieth unto Me from the ground. And now art thou cursed from the earth, which hath opened her mouth to receive thy brother's blood from thy hand; <u>When thou tillest the ground, it shall not henceforth yield unto thee her strength</u>; a fugitive and a vagabond shalt thou be in the earth. And Cain said unto the Lord, My punishment is greater than I can bear."*

Cain was a tiller (farmer) of the ground. Not only was the ground cursed at this time because of Adam's sin, now Cain is unable to farm (cultivate and produce crops) because of his own sin. When he attempts to cultivate the ground, it shall not yield her strength to him causing a famine or scarcity of food for him. He has become a fugitive and a vagabond.

4th Seal – Death and Hell

The Lamb of God opened the fourth seal and the fourth beast said, *"Come and see."* The rider on the pale horse is Death with Hell following him. When Adam sinned in the garden, sin entered into the world and death by sin. Death was passed onward to all men making all men sinners. Death is defined as separation from life in Strong's Concordance #2288 derived from the word "thanatos" meaning death. So when Adam sinned in the garden, mankind became separated from God and began to die physically. To be separated from God is to die spiritually and for the spirit and soul to be separated from the body is physical death. The outward man or body is mortal (subject to death) and slowly perishes day by day.

Hell is an actual place that is located in the earth. The Greek word for hell in this text is Hades. According to Strong's Concordance, Hades is the abode of departed spirits. Before Jesus' physical resurrection from the grave, all mankind went to hell. The uncovenanted man's departed spirit went to the bottom portion of hell and the covenanted man's departed spirit went to the upper portion of hell (the bosom of Abraham) and they were separated by a gulf (Luke 16:19-31). After Jesus's resurrection, the unredeemed man's departed spirit goes to hell at physical death and all born again (redeemed) man's departed spirit goes to heaven to be with the Lord at physical death. All mankind are spirit beings and spirit beings do not die. Only the physical body of a man dies and goes to the grave where it returns to dust (Genesis 3:19). Fallen angels go to hell as well because they are spirit beings. Second Peter 2:4 says, *"For if God spared not the angels that sinned, but cast them down to hell, and delivered them into chains of darkness, to be reserved unto judgment."*

Therefore, hell is a temporary holding place where the sinner's soul and spirit are sent to hell at death waiting for final judgment (the Great White Throne

Judgment). There is coming a future date when death and hell will deliver up the dead which is in them and the dead will be judged according to their works (Revelation 20:11-15). Jesus informs us in Matthew 10:28 when He said, *"And fear not them which kill the body, but are not able to kill the soul: but rather fear Him which is able to destroy both soul and body in hell."*

Before the death and resurrection of Jesus, Satan had the power of death and hell. Jesus conquered death and hell at Calvary or Golgotha on the cross. Hebrews 2:14 says, *"Forasmuch then as the children are partakers of flesh and blood, He also Himself likewise took part of the same; that through death He might destroy him that had the power of death, that is, the devil."* When Adam fell, power was given to them (death and hell) from Satan over a fourth of the earth to kill with weapons of the sword (war), hunger (famine), and death, and beasts (a brute) of the earth. In Genesis chapter 4, there were only four people on the earth at this time. After Cain slew righteous Abel, there were only three people remaining.

The word for "beasts" used in this chapter is "therion" meaning brute of a brutal nature according to Strong's Concordance #2342 and not "behemah" used in Ezekiel the 14th chapter meaning a beast, animal, cattle. Therion is the same word used to describe the Antichrist when referring to him as the beast in Revelation chapters 11 and 13. In Ecclesiastes 3:18 Solomon says, *"I said in mine heart concerning the estate of the sons of men, that God might manifest them, and that they might see that they themselves are beasts."* Therefore, in Ezekiel 14:21 God says, *"For thus saith the Lord God; How much more when I send My four sore judgments upon Jerusalem, the sword, and the famine, and the noisome beast, and the pestilence, to cut off from it man and beast?"* The beast used to kill Abel was Cain influenced by Satan. The sinful nature in Cain caused him to commit murder. Satan, also known as the Destroyer, is used as a vessel to administer these judgments. Isaiah 54:16 the Lord says *"Behold, I have created the smith that bloweth the coals in the fire, and that bringeth forth an instrument for his work; and I have created the waster to destroy."* Jesus confirmed that the devil comes to steal, kill, and destroy (John 10:10).

According to 1st John chapter 3 and verse 12, Cain, the wicked one, slew his brother because his works were evil and his brother's works were righteous. Abel's offering was accepted by the Lord and Cain's was rejected. The blood of righteous Abel cried out to the Lord from the ground. Jesus gives us a better understanding in the 16th chapter of Luke. He gives us an account of two men who died. The beggar, Lazarus, went to the Bosom of Abraham and the rich man went to Hell. Luke 16:19-26 says, *"There was a certain rich man, which was clothed in purple and fine linen, and fared sumptuously every day: And there was a certain beggar named Lazarus, which was laid at his gate, full of sores, And desiring to be fed with the crumbs which fell from the rich man's table: moreover the dogs came and licked his sores. And it came to pass, that the beggar died, and was carried by the angels into Abraham's bosom: the*

Chapter Six

rich man also died, and was buried; And in hell he lift up his eyes, being in torments, and seeth Abraham afar off, and Lazarus in his bosom. And he cried and said, Father Abraham, have mercy on me, and send Lazarus, that he may dip the tip of his finger in water, and cool my tongue; for I am tormented in this flame. But Abraham said, Son, remember that thou in thy lifetime receivedst thy good things, and likewise Lazarus evil things: but now he is comforted, and thou art tormented. And beside all this, between us and you there is a great gulf fixed: so that they which would pass from hence to you cannot; neither can they pass to us, that would come from thence."

At the time of this account, when the righteous died their soul and spirit went into the Bosom of Abraham and the wicked/unrighteous soul and spirit went to Hell. Both of these places were beneath the ground. Jesus lets us know that there was a gulf between these places beneath the ground. The Bosom of Abraham was a place of comfort and Hell is a place full of torment. After Jesus' crucifixion and resurrection, those righteous saints in the Bosom of Abraham ascended with Him into Heaven. The Bosom of Abraham is no longer in the earth but is now located in the third heaven where Christ resides and is called Paradise.

To sum all things up, the promise to the righteous believers in Jesus Christ is to be absent from the body is to be present with the Lord (John 14:1-4 and 2nd Corinthians 5:6-10). The physical body of the righteous person and the unrighteous person returns to dust at their physical death. The soul and spirit of the righteous go to be with the Lord (Ecclesiastes 12:7).

Chapter Six

The righteous must appear before the Judgment Seat of Christ so that every one may receive the things done in his body according to that he has done whether it is good or bad (2nd Corinthians 5:10). The soul and spirit of the unrighteous person go to Hell waiting for The Great White Throne Judgment. Daniel 12:2 states, *"And many of them that sleep in the dust of the earth shall awake, some to everlasting life, and some to shame and everlasting contempt."* **The righteous will awake to everlasting life and the unrighteous to shame and everlasting contempt. There is a day coming when the righteous will receive their glorified bodies at the rapture of the church also known as the catching away of the saints. First Thessalonians 4:13-17 says,** *"But I would not have you to be ignorant, brethren, concerning them which are asleep, that ye sorrow not, even as others which have no hope. For if we believe that Jesus died and rose again, even so them also which sleep in Jesus will God bring with Him. For this we say unto you by the word of the Lord, that we which are alive and remain unto the coming of the Lord shall not prevent them which are asleep. For the Lord Himself shall descend from heaven with a shout, with the voice of the archangel, and with the trump of God: and the dead in Christ shall rise first: Then we which are alive and remain shall be caught up together with them in the clouds, to meet the Lord in the air: and so shall we ever be with the Lord."* **John tells us in 1st John 3:2,** *"Beloved, now are we the sons of God, and it doth not yet appear what we shall be: but we know that, when He shall appear, we shall be like Him; for we shall see Him as He is."*

Chapter Six

Death is the last enemy that will be destroyed (1st Corinthians 15:26). Paul tells us in 1st Corinthians 15:54-57, *"So when this corruptible shall have put on incorruption, and this mortal shall have put on immortality, then shall be brought to pass the saying that is written, Death is swallowed up in victory. O death, where is thy sting? O grave, where is thy victory? The sting of death is sin; and the strength of sin is the law. But thanks be to God, which giveth us the victory through our Lord Jesus Christ."* Death will no longer have a sting and the grave will no longer get the victory because spiritual and physical death will be no longer. The bible tells us that the final resting place for Death and Hell is the Lake of Fire and whosoever name was not found written in the Book of Life was cast into the Lake of Fire.

5th seal – Martyrs

The Lamb of God opened the fifth seal which represents the souls of them that were slain (martyred) for the word of God and for the testimony which they held. They cried with a loud voice, *"How long, O Lord, Holy and True, dost Thou not judge and avenge our blood on them that dwell on the earth?"* White robes were given to them and it was told to them that they should rest for a little season until their fellow servants and their brethren who will be killed as they were killed should be fulfilled. They are currently with the Lord resting and waiting until the last martyr is killed and all things (prophecies) are fulfilled. The white raiment or

Chapter Six

fine linen is the righteous deed and acts of the saints and is a promise to all believers just like when He spoke to the churches in Sardis and Laodicea.

These are some martyred Old Testament saints who were resurrected at the time of Jesus' resurrection. These Old Testament saints have been harvested. The scripture tells us that in Ephesians 4:8-10, *"Wherefore He saith, When He ascended up on high, He led captivity captive, and gave gifts unto men. (Now that He ascended, what is it but that He also descended first into the lower parts of the earth? He that descended is the same also that ascended up far above all heavens, that He might fill all things.)"* They have received their white robes. They are resting in heaven with Jesus until the rapture of the church (remaining OT and NT saints including those martyred) and the fullness of Israel come in to receive their rewards (crowns - Revelation 11:18, 20:4-5, 22:12). The scripture says in 2nd Corinthians 5:10, *"That we must all appear before the judgment seat of Christ; that every one may receive the things done in his body, according to that he hath done, whether it be good or bad."* The Judgment Seat of Christ occurs at Christ's Second Advent.

There will be individuals who will be saved during the great tribulation. Some of them will be martyred because they will not receive the mark of the beast nor worship the Antichrist and his image. These great tribulation saints are a part of the Smyrna church known as the persecuted church.

Chapter Six

At the time of Jesus' Second Advent (physical return to earth – also known as Second Coming), the resurrected Old Testament and resurrected New Testament saints will return with Him to the earth to live in Jerusalem during the Millennium. The fullness of Israel will occur at this time because they will look upon Whom they pierced and mourn (Zechariah 12:10-11).

Once all of these prophecies (events) have been fulfilled, then we will have the Marriage Supper of the Lamb at His Second Coming and His Millennial reign. Jesus said in Luke 22:15-16, 18, 28-30, *"And He said unto them, With desire I have desired to eat this Passover with you before I suffer: For I say unto you, I will not any more eat thereof, until it be fulfilled in the Kingdom of God...For I say unto you, I will not drink of the fruit of the vine, until the Kingdom of God shall come...Ye are they which have continued with Me in My temptations. And I appoint unto you a kingdom, as My Father hath appointed unto Me; That ye may eat and drink at My table in My kingdom, and sit on thrones judging the twelve tribes of Israel"* (Matthew 26:29; Mark 14:25). Jesus was referring to His Millennial Kingdom which is a literal kingdom in which all saints will partake of Communion with Him and then all things will be fulfilled. Of course, we will still be awaiting the New Heaven and the New Earth (New Jerusalem).

6th seal - Pentecost

Chapter Six

The Lamb of God opened the sixth seal which depicts what occurred at Jerusalem when the day of Pentecost was fully come. Jesus' disciples were all with one accord in one place in the upper room. Then suddenly there came a sound from heaven as of a rushing mighty wind and filled the entire house where they were sitting. There was a great earthquake. The sun became black and the moon became as blood. The stars of heaven fell to the earth and the heaven departed as a scroll when it is rolled together. Every mountain and island was moved out of their places. The apostle Peter confirms what happened at Pentecost to be that which was spoken by the prophet Joel in Joel chapter 2. It is written in Acts 2:14-20, *"But Peter, standing up with the eleven, lifted up his voice, and said unto them, Ye men of Judaea, and all ye that dwell at Jerusalem, be this known unto you, and hearken to my words: For these are not drunken, as ye suppose, seeing it is but the third hour (9:00 am) of the day. But this is that which was spoken by the prophet Joel; And it shall come to pass in the last days, saith God, I will pour out of My Spirit upon all flesh: and your sons and your daughters shall prophesy, and your young men shall see visions, and your old men shall dream dreams: And on My servants and on My handmaidens I will pour out in those days of My Spirit; and they shall prophesy: And I will shew wonders in heaven above, and signs in the earth beneath; blood, and fire, and vapour of smoke: The sun shall be turned into darkness, and the moon into blood, before the great and notable day of the Lord come:"*

Chapter Six

The kings of the earth, great men, rich men, chief captains, mighty men, every bondman, and every free man hid themselves in the dens and in the rocks of the mountains. This verse is confirmed in Acts chapter 2:5-12 when it says, *"And there were dwelling at Jerusalem Jews, devout men, out of every nation under heaven. Now when this was noised abroad, the multitude came together, and were confounded, because that every man heard them speak in his own language. And they were all amazed and marvelled, saying one to another, Behold, are not all these which speak Galilaeans? And how hear we every man in our own tongue, wherein we were born? Parthians, and Medes, and Elamites, and the dwellers in Mesopotamia, and in Judaea, and Cappadocia, in Pontus, and Asia, Phrygia, and Pamphylia, in Egypt, and in the parts of Libya about Cyrene, and strangers of Rome, Jews and proselytes, Cretes and Arabians, we do hear them speak in our tongues the wonderful works of God. And they were all amazed, and were in doubt, saying one to another, What meaneth this?"* They said to the mountains and rocks, *"Fall on us, and hide us from the face of Him that sitteth on the throne, and from the wrath of the Lamb: For the great day of His wrath is come; and who shall be able to stand?"* These men thought this event was the Second Advent of Jesus or The Day of the Lord.

CHAPTER SEVEN

144,000 Sealed Prior to the Tribulation & Great Tribulation

After seeing six seals opened, John now sees four angels standing on the four corners of the earth holding the four winds of the earth so that the wind should not blow on the earth, or on the sea, or on any tree. Then, John sees another angel ascending from the east having the seal of the living God. He cried with a loud voice to the four angels of whom it was given to hurt the earth and the sea, saying, *"Hurt not the earth, neither the sea, nor the trees, till We have sealed the servants of our God in their foreheads."* To hurt the earth and the sea are part of the trumpets and vial/bowl (great tribulation) judgments.

I believe that the angel ascending from the east, having the seal of the living God is Jesus because the

Chapter Seven

Lord is the Restrainer and not the church (2nd Thessalonians 2:6-7). *(See The Conclusion For Discussion On The Restrainer.)*

<u>First</u> of all, John makes a point to let us know that the angel is ascending from the east. At Jesus' Ascension in Acts chapter 1, Jesus is ascending in a cloud from the Mount of Olivet (Olives) and two men (angels) in white apparel said, *"Ye men of Galilee, why stand ye gazing up into heaven? This same Jesus, which is taken up from you into heaven, shall so come in like manner as ye have seen Him go into heaven."*

<u>Secondly</u>, this angel has the seal of the living God. A seal represents a mark of ownership, authentication, and protection. These 144,000 believing Jews are sealed with His Holy Spirit which means that they have been purchased by the blood of Jesus, approved of by the Lord, and protected from the kingdom of darkness. They are commissioned to be Christ's effective witnesses in the earth. Jesus said in John 16:13-15, *"Howbeit when He, the Spirit of Truth, is come, He will guide you into all truth: for He shall not speak of Himself; but whatsoever He shall hear, that shall He speak: and He will shew you things to come. He shall glorify Me: for He shall receive of Mine, and shall shew it unto you. All things that the Father hath are Mine: therefore said I, that He shall take of Mine, and shall shew it unto you."* Jesus was also approved by God (Acts 2:22). John also tells us in John 6:27, *"Labour not for the meat which perisheth, but for that meat which endureth unto everlasting life, which the Son of Man shall give unto you: for <u>Him hath God the Father sealed</u>."*

Chapter Seven

At His baptism, the Spirit of God descended upon Him like a dove. Isaiah tells us in chapter 42:1 *"Behold my Servant, Whom I uphold; Mine Elect, in Whom My Soul delighteth; I have put My Spirit upon Him: He shall bring forth judgment (justice) to the Gentiles."*

And <u>thirdly</u>, the angel tells the four angels holding the four winds of the earth to *"Hurt not the earth, neither the sea, nor the trees, till <u>We</u> have sealed the servants of our God in their foreheads."* The "We" that He is referring to is God, the Father, God, the Son, and God, the Holy Spirit, the Blessed Godhead or Trinity. Just like Jesus was sealed by the Father with the Holy Spirit, so are all believers in Jesus. Ephesians 1:13-14 says, *"In Whom ye also trusted, after that ye heard the word of truth, the gospel of your salvation: in Whom also after that ye believed, ye were sealed with that Holy Spirit of Promise, which is the earnest of our inheritance until the redemption of the purchased possession, unto the praise of His glory."*

Twelve thousand Israelites from each tribe were sealed totaling a hundred and forty-four thousand from the children of Israel. These hundred and forty-four thousand are Israelites who follow God and the Lamb. The scripture states in Revelation the 14th chapter that these were redeemed from the earth being the first fruits to God and to the Lamb. They were not defiled with women and follow the Lamb wherever He goes and in their mouth was found no guile. They are without fault (blameless) before the throne of God because they have been justified.

Chapter Seven

Multitude From the Great Tribulation in White Robes

After this John beheld and saw a great multitude which no man could number of all nations, kindreds, people, and tongues, which stood before the throne and before the Lamb clothed with white robes and palms branches in their hands. They cried with a loud voice saying, *"Salvation to our God which sitteth upon the throne, and unto the Lamb."* All of the angels that stood around the throne, along with the elders and the four beasts, fell before the throne on their faces and worshipped God saying, *"Amen: Blessing, and glory, and wisdom, and thanksgiving, and honour, and power, and might, be unto our God for ever and ever. Amen."* Then one of the elders answered saying to John, *"What are these which are arrayed in white robes? and whence came they?"* John said to him, *"Sir, thou knowest."* He said to John, *"These are they which came out of great tribulation, and have washed their robes, and made them white in the blood of the Lamb. Therefore are they before the throne of God, and serve Him day and night in His temple: and He that sitteth on the throne shall dwell among them. They shall hunger no more, neither thirst any more; neither shall the sun light on them, nor any heat. For the Lamb which is in the midst of the throne shall feed them, and shall lead them unto living fountains of waters: and God shall wipe away all tears from their eyes."*

CHAPTER EIGHT

7th seal- Pentecost

The seventh seal is opened and there is silence in heaven about thirty minutes. This silence is a time of uninterrupted speech.

John sees seven angels standing before God and to them were given seven trumpets. Another angel comes and stands at the altar having a golden censer. There was given to Him much incense so that He would offer the incense with the prayers of all saints upon the golden altar which was before the throne. The smoke of the incense which came with the prayers of the saints ascended up before God out of the angel's hand. The angel took the censer and filled it with fire from the altar and cast it into the earth. There were voices, thundering, lightning, and an earthquake.

This event takes place in the third heaven. The angel with the golden censer is Christ and He is the reason for the silence. Habakkuk 2:20 says, *"But the Lord is in His Holy Temple: let all the earth keep silence before Him."* He has been given much incense along with the prayers of the saints to offer upon the golden altar before the throne. The smoke of the incense which came with the prayers of the saints ascended up before God out of Christ's hand. Then, Christ took the censer and filled it with Fire from the altar and cast it into the earth. Then, there were voices, and thundering, and lightning, and an earthquake.

This event is Christ sending the Holy Spirit (also referred to as the Promise of the Father, the Comforter, and the Spirit of Truth) into the earth on the day of Pentecost (known as the outpouring of the Holy Spirit). The Holy Spirit is also known as the Fire of God in which He purifies and purges the saints (Matthew 3:11-12; Luke 3:16-17). The scripture states in Luke 12:49-50, *"I am come to send Fire on the earth; and what will I, if it be already kindled? But I have a baptism to be baptized with; and how Am I straitened till it be accomplished!"* And in John 16:7, *"Nevertheless I tell you the truth; It is expedient for you that I go away: for if I go not away, the Comforter will not come unto you; but if I depart, I will send Him unto you."*

Chapter Eight

In Acts chapter one, the disciples are told by Jesus, the Christ, to wait for the Promise of the Father and that they will receive power after that the Holy Ghost is come upon them to be witnesses of Him both in Jerusalem, in Judaea, in Samaria, and to the uttermost part of the earth. While they were waiting, they all continued in one accord in prayer and supplication with the women, Mary, the mother of Jesus, and with His brethren.

In Acts chapter two, when the day of Pentecost fully came, they were all with one accord in one place. Then suddenly there came a sound from heaven as of a rushing mighty wind and filled the entire house where they were sitting. And there appeared to them cloven (divided) tongues like as of fire and sat upon each of them. And they were <u>all filled</u> with the Holy Ghost and began to speak with other tongues as the Spirit gave them utterance. Peter tells us that this is that which was spoken by the prophet Joel, *"And it shall come to pass in the last days, saith God, I will pour out of My Spirit upon all flesh: and your sons and your daughters shall prophesy, and your young men shall see visions, and your old men shall dream dreams: And on My servants and on My handmaidens I will pour out in those days of My Spirit; and they shall prophesy: ... This promise is unto you, and to your children, and to all that are afar off, even as many as the LORD our God shall call."* This event is the initial outpouring of the Holy Ghost into the earth on Jesus' disciples (believers) and is called the Feast of Pentecost or Feast of Weeks (a Feast of the

Chapter Eight

Lord). The initial outpouring into the earth occurred only once because the scripture says when the day of Pentecost was fully come.

Believers are still experiencing Pentecost (the Outpouring of the Holy Spirit) because men are still being saved and filled with the Holy Ghost with the evidence of speaking in tongues and will continue to be filled with the Holy Spirit until Jesus comes. When Jesus comes, we will no longer know in part. We will see Him face to face along with the nation of Israel (1st John 3:2). First Corinthians 13:8-12 says, *"Charity never faileth: but whether there be prophecies, they shall fail; whether there be tongues, they shall cease; whether there be knowledge, it shall vanish away. For we know in part, and we prophesy in part. But when that which is perfect is come, then that which is in part shall be done away. When I was a child, I spake as a child, I understood as a child, I thought as a child: but when I became a man, I put away childish things. For now we see through a glass, darkly; but then face to face: now I know in part; but then shall I know even as also I am known. And now abideth faith, hope, charity, these three; but the greatest of these is charity."* Therefore, in the Millennium, we will know all things and be free from Satan's schemes (Revelation 11:15; Zechariah 14:16-19). In the New Heaven and New Earth (New Jerusalem), we will not remember any of the former things in this earth (Revelation 21:4). Then, we will see the Father and the Lamb face to face (Revelation 22:4).

Chapter Eight

The evidence part of speaking in tongues is that all 120 disciples were each speaking in a different language unknown to them but known to those of other countries in Jerusalem who were present. They heard them speaking the wonderful works of God in their language (Acts 2:3-11; 1st Corinthians 14:24-25). A language unknown to each of the disciples, but known to those present. Isaiah refers to these tongues as stammering tongues in Isaiah 28:11-12 which says, *"For with stammering lips and another tongue will He speak to this people. To Whom He said, This is the rest wherewith ye may cause the weary to rest; and this is the refreshing: yet they would not hear."*

This promise and gift are to all believers as many as the Lord, our God, will call. In 1st Corinthians 14:21-22, it says that tongues are for the believer and a sign to the unbeliever. He that speaks in an unknown tongue speaks not to men, but to God, he edifies himself, and with the interpretation of tongues, the church is edified (1st Corinthians 14; Jude 1:20). He is also our Intercessor because we know not what to pray for (Romans 8:26-27).

The Father (Holy Spirit) draws the unbeliever to Jesus when he hears the gospel of grace preached. The scripture says no man can come to the Father unless the Father (Holy Spirit) draws them (John 6:44; Romans 10:13-15). The Holy Spirit indwells and baptizes the believer immediately into the body of Christ the exact

Chapter Eight

moment of their belief in Jesus Christ and His finished works (death, burial, resurrection). At salvation, the believer receives all nine gifts of the Holy Spirit. These gifts are manifested by the Holy Spirit dividing to every man as He wills. First Corinthians 12:7-13 says, *"But the manifestation of the Spirit is given to every man to profit withal. For to one is given by the Spirit the word of wisdom; to another the word of knowledge by the same Spirit; To another faith by the same Spirit; to another the gifts of healing by the same Spirit; To another the working of miracles; to another prophecy; to another discerning of spirits; to another divers kinds of tongues; to another the interpretation of tongues: But all these worketh that one and the selfsame Spirit, dividing to every man severally as He will. For as the body is one, and hath many members, and all the members of that one body, being many, are one body: so also is Christ. For by one Spirit are we all baptized into one body, whether we be Jews or Gentiles, whether we be bond or free; and have been all made to drink into one Spirit."*

Jesus is the One Who baptizes the believer with the Holy Spirit and the evidence of speaking in tongues. Every believer has the gift to speak in tongues, but not all will speak in tongues (1st Corinthians 14:5). This is a two-fold (double) blessing available to every believer. The indwelling of the Holy Spirit occurs immediately and remains once the believer hears the gospel and believes in his heart on Jesus.

The filling (outpouring of the Holy Spirit) is the controlling influence of the Holy Spirit within the believer. Ephesians 5:18 says, *"And be not drunk with wine, wherein is excess; but be filled with the Spirit."* The filling will never occur before the indwelling of the Holy Spirit. It is always after the indwelling of the Holy Spirit. Remember that the indwelling of the Holy Spirit occurs once and is permanent. The filling of the Holy Spirit can occur more than once and is forever, continually, and ongoing within the believer (Acts 4:31, Ephesians 5:18).

Sometimes the filling occurs immediately and simultaneously with the indwelling. In Acts 10:44-46, *"While Peter yet spake these words, the Holy Ghost fell on all them which heard the word. And they of the circumcision which believed were astonished, as many as came with Peter, because that on the Gentiles also was poured out the gift of the Holy Ghost. For they heard them speak with tongues, and magnify God..."*

Sometimes the filling occurs by the laying on of hands. In Acts 19:6, *"And when Paul had laid his hands upon them, the Holy Ghost came on them; and they spake with tongues, and prophesied."*

And sometimes the filling will occur sometime later *just like* it did for the disciples in Acts chapter 2 during worship.

The Day the Church Began

Some believe Pentecost to be the date that the church began, but it is not. Pentecost is the initial outpouring of the Holy Spirit into the earth. The date the church began is recorded in Luke chapter 4 when Jesus read

Chapter Eight

from the book of Isaiah the 61st chapter and said, *"The Spirit of the Lord is upon Me, because He hath anointed Me to preach the gospel to the poor; He hath sent Me to heal the brokenhearted, to preach deliverance to the captives, and recovering of sight to the blind, to set at liberty them that are bruised, To preach the acceptable year of the Lord...This day is this scripture fulfilled in your ears."* He then proceeded to choose His twelve apostles (disciples). Jesus asked His disciples one day *"Whom do men say that I the Son of Man Am? And whom say ye that I Am?"* Simon Peter responded, *"Thou art the Christ, the Son of the living God. And Jesus answered and said unto him, Blessed art thou, Simon Barjona: for flesh and blood hath not revealed it unto thee, but My Father which is in heaven. And I say also unto thee, That thou art Peter, and upon this rock I will build My church; and the gates of hell shall not prevail against it* (Matthew 16:13-23; Mark 8:27-33)."

Jesus is telling His disciples that upon a person's belief and confession of faith (statement of truth), men are saved. Luke chapter 4 occurred before Jesus' crucifixion and resurrection from the dead. The disciples were saved because they believed on Jesus as the Christ. Jesus said in Luke 17:21 that the kingdom of God is within you and in your midst. This statement was made prior to His death, burial, and resurrection. It is the rule of God in the hearts of men. Romans 14:17-18 says, *"For the kingdom of God is not meat and drink; but righteousness, and peace, and joy in the Holy Ghost. For he that in these things serveth Christ is acceptable to God, and approved of men."* It is your

Chapter Eight

believing and confession of faith that saves a person just like Rahab (Joshua 2:9-14) and Ruth (Ruth 1:16-17) confessions of faith were before Jesus's death on the cross and resurrection. Both of these women were Gentiles who appears in the lineage of Jesus in Matthew chapter 1 verse 5. They both believed in the God of Israel.

Jesus (The Bridegroom) has power on earth to forgive sin. Matthew 9:5-6, *"For whether is easier, to say, Thy sins be forgiven thee; or to say, Arise, and walk? But that ye may know that the Son of Man hath power on earth to forgive sins, (then saith He to the sick of the palsy,) Arise, take up thy bed, and go unto thine house."*

He is God, the Father, in the flesh and that is what He told Philip in John 14:8-11, *"Philip saith unto Him, Lord, show us the Father, and it sufficeth us. Jesus saith unto him, Have I been so long time with you, and yet hast thou not known Me, Philip? he that hath seen Me hath seen the Father; and how sayest thou then, Show us the Father? Believest thou not that I am in the Father, and the Father in Me? the words that I speak unto you I speak not of Myself: but the Father that dwelleth in Me, He doeth the works. Believe Me that I am in the Father, and the Father in Me: or else believe Me for the very works' sake."*

There are others, in the gospels, whose sins were forgiven and saved prior to the cross. The woman with the alabaster box in Luke 7:37-50 and a certain blind man in Luke 18:35-43 are some examples.

Chapter Eight

The Woman with the Alabaster Box

Luke 7:37-38, 48-50 *"And, behold, a woman in the city, which was a sinner, when she knew that Jesus sat at meat in the Pharisee's house, brought an alabaster box of ointment, and stood at His feet behind Him weeping, and began to wash His feet with tears, and did wipe them with the hairs of her head, and kissed His feet, and anointed them with the ointment. And He said unto her, Thy sins are forgiven. And they that sat at meat with Him began to say within themselves, Who is this that forgiveth sins also? And He said to the woman, Thy faith hath saved thee; go in peace."*

A Certain Blind Man

Luke 18:41-42 reads, *"Saying, What wilt thou that I shall do unto thee? And he said, Lord, that I may receive my sight. And Jesus said unto him, Receive thy sight: thy faith hath saved thee."*

The scripture says in John 5:24, *"Verily, verily, I say unto you, He that heareth My word, and believeth on Him that sent Me, hath everlasting life, and shall not come into condemnation; but is passed from death unto life."*

The question now being asked is, "If Jesus could forgive sin while on earth, then why did He have to die on the cross? One of the reasons why He died a sinner's death on the cross is to destroy all the works of the devil (sin and death). Another reason why is because without the shedding of His blood there is no forgiveness of sin. Prior to the cross, the blood of clean animals without

Chapter Eight

blemish (representing no sin or blameless) was shed or sacrificed which could only cover their sin for a year.

And another reason why is because He was leaving the earth and did not want to leave us comfortless and to give us the Holy Spirit, with all nine spiritual gifts, as a Helper. While in the earth and in a physical body, Jesus could only be in one geographical location at a time which was His only limitation. He walked alongside of his disciples as the Parakletos. Parakletos is a term used to refer to the Holy Spirit and it means summoned, called to one's side, especially called to one's aid. He is Jesus in another person (The Father, Who is the Holy Spirit).

The Holy Spirit indwells us and helps us. He will never leave us nor forsake us. He is not limited to the restriction of an earthly body because the body is subject to the environment in which it was created. John 16:7 says, *"Nevertheless I tell you the truth; It is expedient for you that I go away: for if I go not away, the Comforter will not come unto you; but if I depart, I will send Him unto you. And when He is come, He will reprove the world of sin, and of righteousness, and of judgment: Of sin, because they believe not on Me; Of righteousness, because I go to My Father, and ye see Me no more; Of judgment, because the prince of this world is judged."* Jesus, being the Father, sent us another Comforter Who is the Holy Spirit or Holy Ghost. They are all One and the Same. We now have Jesus, the Father, dwelling in us in another person as the Holy Spirit.

Chapter Eight

(For An Explanation Of The Triune Godhead – See The Holy Trinity – The Triune God)

After the cross, we have an example of believing on the Lord Jesus to be saved in Acts 16:25-34, *"And at midnight Paul and Silas prayed, and sang praises unto God: and the prisoners heard them. And suddenly there was a great earthquake, so that the foundations of the prison were shaken: and immediately all the doors were opened, and every one's bands were loosed. And the keeper of the prison awaking out of his sleep, and seeing the prison doors open, he drew out his sword, and would have killed himself, supposing that the prisoners had been fled. But Paul cried with a loud voice, saying, Do thyself no harm: for we are all here. Then he called for a light, and sprang in, and came trembling, and fell down before Paul and Silas, And brought them out, and said, Sirs, <u>what must I do to be saved?</u> And they said, <u>Believe on the Lord Jesus Christ, and thou shalt be saved, and thy house.</u> And they spake unto him the word of the Lord, and to all that were in his house. And he took them the same hour of the night, and washed their stripes; and was baptized, he and all his, straightway. And when he had brought them into his house, he set meat before them, and rejoiced, believing in God with all his house."*

Romans 10:9-13, *"That if thou shalt confess with thy mouth the Lord Jesus, and shalt believe in thine heart that God hath raised Him from the dead, thou shalt be saved. For with the heart man believeth unto righteousness; and with the mouth confession is made unto salvation. For the scripture saith, Whosoever*

Chapter Eight

believeth on Him shall not be ashamed. For there is no difference between the Jew and the Greek: for the same Lord over all is rich unto all that call upon Him. For whosoever shall call upon the name of the Lord shall be saved."

Simon Peter denied the Lord three times before the rooster crowed because of Satan's sifting. Jesus prayed that Peter's faith fail not and told Peter that when he is converted to strengthen his brethren. In Luke 22:31-32, *"And the Lord said, Simon, Simon, behold, Satan hath desired to have you, that he may sift you as wheat: But I have prayed for thee, that thy faith fail not: and when thou art converted, strengthen thy brethren."* **Matthew 26:31-35 says,** *"Then saith Jesus unto them, All ye shall be offended because of Me this night: for it is written, I will smite the Shepherd, and the sheep of the flock shall be scattered abroad. But after I am risen again, I will go before you into Galilee. Peter answered and said unto Him, Though all men shall be offended because of Thee, yet will I never be offended. Jesus said unto him, Verily I say unto thee, That this night, before the cock crow, thou shalt deny Me thrice. Peter said unto Him, Though I should die with Thee, yet will I not deny Thee. Likewise also said all the disciples."* **In the Strong's Concordance, the word "offend" is skandalizó and means "to put a snare in the way, hence to cause to stumble (fall away).**

After Jesus resurrection from the dead, He breathed on His disciples and told them to receive the Holy Ghost because all of them were offended. Peter is the only disciple that denied Him three times before men in the

scripture. Peter is later converted and restored by Jesus and asked three times if he loved Him and was told to feed and tend His sheep. *"So when they had dined, Jesus saith to Simon Peter, Simon, son of Jonas, lovest thou Me more than these? He saith unto Him, Yea, Lord; Thou knowest that I love Thee. He saith unto him, Feed My lambs. He saith to him again the second time, Simon, son of Jonas, lovest thou Me? He saith unto Him, Yea, Lord; Thou knowest that I love Thee. He saith unto him, Feed My sheep. He saith unto him the third time, Simon, son of Jonas, lovest thou Me? Peter was grieved because He said unto him the third time, Lovest thou Me? And he said unto Him, Lord, Thou knowest all things; Thou knowest that I love thee. Jesus saith unto him, Feed My sheep"* (John 21:15-17).

It is written in Revelation 12:11, *"And they overcame him (Satan) by the blood of the Lamb, and by the word of their testimony; and they loved not their lives unto the death."* We are not ashamed to be identified with Jesus and are willing participants in His sufferings. First Peter 4:16-19 says, *"Yet if any man suffer as a Christian, let him not be ashamed; but let him glorify God on this behalf. For the time is come that judgment must begin at the house of God: and if it first begin at us, what shall the end be of them that obey not the gospel of God? And if the righteous scarcely be saved, where shall the ungodly and the sinner appear? Wherefore let them that suffer according to the will of God commit the keeping of their souls to Him in well doing, as unto a faithful Creator."* Second Timothy 2:12-13 says, *"If we suffer, we shall also reign with Him: if we deny Him, He also will deny us: If we believe not, yet He abideth faithful: He cannot deny Himself."* In Romans 1:16, *"For I am not ashamed of the gospel of Christ: for it is the power of God unto salvation to every one that believeth; to the Jew first, and also to the Greek..."*

Jesus also tells Peter that where Peter did not want to go on the night in which Jesus was betrayed, he will eventually go. The scripture says in John 21:18-19, *"Verily, verily, I say unto thee, When thou wast young, thou girdest thyself, and walkedst whither thou wouldest: but when thou shalt be old, thou shalt stretch forth thy hands, and another shall gird thee, and carry thee whither thou wouldest not. This spake He, signifying by what death he (Peter) should glorify God. And when He had spoken this, He saith unto him, Follow Me."* Jesus was letting Peter know that on the night when Jesus was betrayed, Satan wanted to crucify Peter along with Jesus. He was also letting Peter know that a day was approaching when he is old that Peter would be crucified for Jesus' sake and the gospel. He also was letting him know that no matter what his end will be, continue to follow Christ faithfully even to the death on the cross.

The Seven Trumpets (Is)

The seven angels who had the seven trumpets prepared themselves to sound. This event is called the Feast of Trumpets which occurs in the seventh month during harvest time. Some ask, "Where are we on God's calendar of events?" We are in the Feast of

Chapter Eight

Trumpets. It is a memorial of the blowing of trumpets and a holy convocation. It is a time of harvesting of Jews and Gentiles that believe on Jesus' finished works as well as a time of sorrow, suffering, and tribulation (not the great tribulation).

For further explanation - See Leviticus 23 - The Feasts of the Lord (Trumpets)

1st Trumpet

The first trumpet sounds and hail and fire mingled with blood were poured upon the earth. A third of the trees were burned and all green grasses were burned.

2nd Trumpet

The second trumpet sounds and what appears to be as a great mountain burning with fire was poured into the seas. A third of the sea became as blood, a third of the creatures in the sea died, and a third of the ships in the sea were destroyed. **This appears to be the attack on Pearl Harbor in 1941.**

3rd Trumpet

The third trumpet sounds and a great star (Wormwood) from heaven, burning as it were a lamp, fell upon the third of the rivers and upon the fountains of waters. A third of the waters became wormwood (bitter) and many men died of the waters because they were made bitter.

Chapter Eight

4*th* Trumpet

The fourth trumpet sounds, and a third of the sun was smitten, and a third of the moon, and a third of the stars, were darkened. The day was without light for a third of the day and the night likewise.

After the first four trumpets sounds, John sees and hears an angel flying through the midst of heaven saying with a loud voice, *"Woe, woe, woe, to the inhabiters of the earth by reason of the other voices of the trumpet of the three angels, which are yet to sound!"* **The angel is warning of the three other trumpets judgment which is yet to sound.**

CHAPTER NINE

5th Trumpet

¹ And the fifth angel sounded, and I saw a star fall from heaven unto the earth: and to him was given the key of the bottomless pit.

² And he opened the bottomless pit; and there arose a smoke out of the pit, as the smoke of a great furnace; and the sun and the air were darkened by reason of the smoke of the pit.

³ And there came out of the smoke locusts upon the earth: and unto them was given power, as the scorpions of the earth have power.

⁴ And it was commanded them that they should not hurt the grass of the earth, neither any green thing, neither

Chapter Nine

any tree; but only those men which have not the seal of God in their foreheads.

⁵ And to them it was given that they should not kill them, but that they should be tormented five months: and their torment was as the torment of a scorpion, when he striketh a man.

⁶ And in those days shall men seek death, and shall not find it; and shall desire to die, and death shall flee from them.

⁷ And the shapes of the locusts were like unto horses prepared unto battle; and on their heads were as it were crowns like gold, and their faces were as the faces of men.

⁸ And they had hair as the hair of women, and their teeth were as the teeth of lions.

⁹ And they had breastplates, as it were breastplates of iron; and the sound of their wings was as the sound of chariots of many horses running to battle.

¹⁰ And they had tails like unto scorpions, and there were stings in their tails: and their power was to hurt men five months.

¹¹ And they had a king over them, which is the angel of the bottomless pit, whose name in the Hebrew tongue is Abaddon, but in the Greek tongue hath his name Apollyon.

¹² One woe is past; and, behold, there come two woes more hereafter.

Chapter Nine

The fifth trumpet sound. This trumpet appears to be the Persian Gulf War. The ground troops fought for five months. During this war, Iraqi military forces ignited fires to the oil wells in Kuwait causing tremendous amounts of smoke. This smoke traveled around the entire globe. The war ended with military strikes and a cease-fire agreement was signed. The approved airstrikes were performed by the fourth beast in Daniel chapter 7:7 which is The Headquarters of the United Nations Security Council located in New York City, New York in the United States of America.

The Headquarters of the United Nations is located in the city known as Mystery Babylon and Babel means confusion. The word, confusion, is associated with the tower of Babel in Genesis chapter 11 which was located in Shinar (Babylon). We know where the confusion comes from. It comes from Satan. Satan is the author of confusion. First Corinthians 14:33 says, *"For God is not the author of confusion, but of peace, as in all churches of the saints."* He is the god of this world (John 12:31).

The Headquarters of the United Nations is figuratively the breastplates of iron mentioned in this chapter. The Headquarters of the United Nations is not evil. It is just that they are a one-world governmental body trying to bring and keep world-wide peace among nations. The United Nations (UN) Security Council is the military forces of the UN as to determining peaceful resolutions. They vote on international issues and determine whether to bring peace and prosperity by rendering aid, sanctions, or war to a nation or nations. Psalm 33:12 says, *"Blessed is the nation whose God is the Lord; and the people Whom He hath chosen for His Own inheritance."* God never intended for peace and prosperity to come to men through the works of the man's flesh. Jesus, the Prince of Peace, can only bring true peace and deliverance to men through world-wide evangelism. They are doing the same thing as they were doing in Genesis Chapter 11 with the tower of Babel. Men building a city (New York City), a tower (fortress), and coming together in agreement as in a one-world type of government. They were all, at that time, of one language and of one speech depicting unity. There is nothing wrong with being unified. God wants us to unified in His Son and for genuine love to be the motivating factor of our actions which will bring about godly peace.

In this chapter, they have a king over them, which is the angel of the bottomless pit, whose name in the Hebrew tongue is Abaddon, but in the Greek tongue, his name is Apollyon. In the Strong's Concordance, Abaddon means "Destroyer" (i.e. Destroying Angel or place of destruction (personified) and we know that Satan is known as the Destroyer (Exodus 12:23; Hebrews 11:28). There is a city in Iran named Abadan and it resides on Abadan Island where a war was previously fought with Iraq in the decade prior to the Persian Gulf War.

Chapter Nine

The first woe is completed. There are two more to come.

6*th* Trumpet

The sixth trumpet sounds and a voice from the four horns of the golden altar which is before God said to the sixth angel, *"Loose the four angels which are bound in the great river Euphrates."* These four angels were loosed, which were prepared for an hour, a day, a month, and a year, to slay a third of men by fire, smoke, and brimstone which issued out of their mouths. The size of the army will be 200 million soldiers having breastplates of fire, jacinth, and brimstone (color of sulfur or sulphur). This army has the heads of lions. Their power is in their mouth and in their tails. Their tails were like serpents and with them, they do inflict hurt.

This is another war that will be fought in the future. According to the description given, this army is China. The colors associated with this army's breastplate of fire are the same as colors in a flame of fire. The flag reflects the old Chinese Qing Dynasty from 1889 to 1912. That empire collapsed in 1912 which fits the description of the army in this chapter. A picture of this flag is in World Book Encyclopedia, 1989, Flag Section, Page 205. You can also search online to see this flag.

Chapter Nine

The scripture continues to say in verses 20-21, *"And the rest of the men which were not killed by these plagues yet repented not of the works of their hands, that they should not worship devils, and idols of gold, and silver, and brass, and stone, and of wood: which neither can see, nor hear, nor walk: Neither repented they of their murders, nor of their sorceries, nor of their fornication, nor of their thefts."*

CHAPTER TEN

John sees a mighty angel or Christ, the Lion of the tribe of Judah, descended from heaven, clothed with a cloud and a rainbow was upon His head. His face was as the sun and His feet as pillars of fire. He had in His hand a little book that was opened. He set His right foot upon the sea and His left foot on the earth. He cried with a loud voice as when a lion roars. When He had cried the seven thunders uttered their voices. The seven thunders is God, the Father, speaking just like the seven Spirits are a reference to the Holy Spirit (John 12:27-30; Revelation 4:6; Isaiah 11:2-3; Psalm 18:13; 29; 1st Samuel 2:10; 2nd Samuel 22:14; Job 37:4-5). The thundering is the Father's voice reverberating. Seven is the number of perfection or completeness and is always associated with the Godhead (James 1:17 & 25). They alone are perfection. John was about to write what the seven thunders had uttered and heard a voice from

Chapter Ten

heaven saying, *"Seal up those things which the seven thunders uttered, and write them not."* Then, the angel which was standing upon the sea and upon the earth lifted up His hand to heaven and swore by Him that lives forever and ever Who created the heaven, the earth, the sea, and the things in each of them. He swore that there should be time no longer when the voice of the seventh angel begins to sound and the mystery of God should be finished as He hath declared to His servants the prophets (Revelation 11:15).

Paul tells us this mystery in Ephesians 1:9-14, *"Having <u>made known unto us the mystery of His will</u>, according to His good pleasure which He hath purposed in Himself: That <u>in the dispensation of the fullness of times He might gather together in one all things in Christ, both which are in heaven, and which are on earth; even in Him</u>: In Whom also we have obtained an inheritance, being predestinated according to the purpose of Him Who worketh all things after the counsel of His own will: That we should be to the praise of His glory, who first trusted in Christ. In Whom ye also trusted, after that ye heard the word of truth, the gospel of your salvation: in Whom also after that ye believed, ye were sealed with that Holy Spirit of promise, which is the earnest of our inheritance until the redemption of the purchased possession, unto the praise of His glory."* And in Ephesians 3:2-6, *"If ye have heard of the dispensation of the grace of God which is given me to you-ward: How that by revelation He made known unto me <u>the mystery</u>; (as I wrote afore in few words, Whereby, when ye read, ye may understand my knowledge in the mystery of Christ) Which in other ages*

Chapter Ten

was not made known unto the sons of men, as it <u>is now revealed</u> unto His holy apostles and prophets by the Spirit; <u>That the Gentiles should be fellowheirs, and of the same body, and partakers of His promise in Christ by the gospel.</u>" Therefore, the mystery is the church consisting of believing Jews and Gentiles. *(See Chapter 4 - Declaring The End From The Beginning.)*

The voice which John heard from heaven spoke to him again and said, *"Go and take the little book which is open in the hand of the angel which standeth upon the sea and upon the earth."* John went to the angel and said, *"Give me the little book."* Then, the angel said, *"Take it, and eat it up; and it shall make thy belly bitter, but it shall be in thy mouth sweet as honey."* Then, John took the little book out of the angel's hand and ate. It was sweet as honey and made John's belly bitter. Then, he said to John, *"Thou must prophesy again before many peoples, and nations, and tongues, and kings."* This statement is proof why the rapture did not occur in Revelation chapter 4 when God said to John, *"Come up hither, and I will shew thee things which must be hereafter. And immediately I was in the spirit: and, behold, a throne was set in heaven, and One sat on the throne."* If the rapture of the church occurred in Revelation chapter 4, then we as the current day church missed the rapture. Therefore, we know that the rapture of the church has not occurred.

This chapter brings clarity to this thought process because John was sent back and told to prophesy. He did not remain in the third heaven where God and

Chapter Ten

Christ now reside. The rapture of the church will occur at the sound of the 7th (last) trumpet when the mystery of God will be finished and time is no longer. The mystery of God is found in Ephesian 1:9-10 and in Ephesians 3:2-6. When the seventh angel sounds the seventh trumpet, great voices in heaven rejoices by saying, *"The kingdoms of this world are become the kingdoms of our Lord and of His Christ; and He shall reign for ever and ever"* **(Revelation 11:15).**

CHAPTER ELEVEN

Two Witnesses

There was given to John a reed like a measuring rod. The angel stood and said, *"Rise, and measure the temple of God, and the altar, and them that worship therein. But the court which is without the temple leave out, and measure it not; for it is given unto the Gentiles: and the holy city shall they tread under foot forty and two months. And I will give power unto my two witnesses, and they shall prophesy a thousand two hundred and threescore days, clothed in sackcloth."* These are the two olive trees and the two candlesticks standing before the God of the earth. If any man will hurt them, a fire will proceed out of their mouth and devour their enemies. If any man will hurt them, that man must be killed in the same

Chapter Eleven

manner. They have the power to shut the heaven so that it does not rain during the days of their prophesy. They also have power over the waters to turn them into blood and to smite the earth with all plagues as often as they will. When they have finished their testimony, the beast that ascends out of the bottomless pit shall make war against them, overcome and kill them. Their dead bodies shall lie in the street of Jerusalem, which spiritually is called Sodom and Egypt, where also our Lord was crucified. People, kindred's, tongues, and nations shall see their dead bodies for three and a half days and will not allow their dead bodies to be put in graves. They that dwell upon the earth shall rejoice over them and be merry. They shall send gifts one to another because these two prophets tormented them that dwell in the earth. After three and a half days, the Spirit of Life from God enters into them and they stand upon their feet. Great fear fell upon them which saw them. They heard a great voice from heaven saying to them, *"Come up hither"* and they ascended into heaven in a cloud and their enemies beheld them. At the same hour, there was a great earthquake and a tenth of the city fell. The earthquake caused seven thousands of the men to be slain and the remnants were frightened and gave glory to the God of heaven. The second woe (sixth trumpet) is past and the third woe is coming quickly.

Who are these two olive trees? Zechariah 4:14 tells us that these are the two anointed ones that stand by the Lord of the whole earth. Most of the church believes that they are Moses and Elijah. They represent the law (Moses) and the prophets (Elijah). The miracles that these two witnesses will perform in this chapter are the same as those that Moses and Elijah performed in the Old Testament. Moses and Elijah were both on the mountain of transfiguration in spirit form (a spiritual body) with Jesus. When Jesus was transfigured, Peter, James, and John were actual eyewitnesses who saw these two prophets talking with Jesus. Peter confirmed his witness in the book of 2nd Peter 1:16-18 when he said, *"For we have not followed cunningly devised fables, when we made known unto you the power and coming of our Lord Jesus Christ, but were eyewitnesses of His majesty. For He received from God the Father honour and glory, when there came such a voice to Him from The Excellent Glory, This is My beloved Son, in Whom I Am well pleased. And this voice which came from heaven we heard, when we were with Him in the holy mount."*

I believe for sure that they are Elijah and Moses because the scripture says they are in Malachi 3:1, *"Behold, I will send <u>my messenger</u>, and he shall prepare the way before Me: and the Lord, Whom ye seek, shall suddenly come to His temple, <u>even the messenger of the covenant</u>, whom ye delight in: behold, he shall come, saith the Lord of hosts.."*

To prepare the way always refers to the spirit of Elijah or Elijah himself (Luke 3:2-6; Matthew 3:3, 11:9-15). The spirit of Elijah or Elijah always comes before Christ to restore all things or prepare the way for the Messiah. In Matthew 17:10-13 it says, *"And His disciples asked Him saying, Why then say the scribes that Elias (Elijah) must first come? And Jesus answered and said unto them, Elias (Elijah) truly shall first come, and restore all things. But I say unto you, That Elias (Elijah) is come already, and they knew him not, but have done unto him whatsoever they listed. Likewise shall also the Son of Man suffer of them. Then the disciples understood that He spake unto them of John the Baptist."* Therefore, John the Baptist came in the spirit of Elijah before Jesus' earthly ministry. John the Baptist was beheaded by Herod Antipas.

Malachi 4:5-6 says, *"Behold, I will send you Elijah the prophet before the coming of the great and dreadful day of the Lord: And he shall turn the heart of the fathers to the children, and the heart of the children to their fathers, lest I come and smite the earth with a curse."* Elijah, in spirit form, ministered to Jesus on the mount of transfiguration before His crucifixion, death, and resurrection (Matthew 17:1-8; Mark 9:1-8). Jesus was transfigured before them and His face did shine as the Sun and His raiment was white as light. After Jesus' resurrection and ascension, many resurrected Old Testament saints ascended with Him (Matthew 27:52-53; Ezekiel 37:1-14; Acts 2:29; 1st Corinthians 15:35-50; Ephesians 4:8-10). The remaining Old Testament saints will be resurrected at Christ's Second Coming in the air with the New Testament saints. On the day of Pentecost, the Holy Spirit, another Comforter, was poured into the earth.

One of the witnesses in this chapter is Elijah, in a physical body, which will be persecuted, rejected, killed, and resurrected prior to Jesus coming in the air for His church at the seventh trumpet also known as the rapture of the church. Elijah will not be able to turn the hearts of the fathers to the children and the heart of the children to their fathers because the scripture says that these two prophets tormented them that dwelt on the earth. God gave them the power to hurt and kill those that were trying to hurt and kill them in the same manner. Therefore, Elijah will come three and a half years before the rapture of the New Testament saints, then the great tribulation, then Jesus Second Coming or Advent. The great tribulation is the *"lest I come and smite the earth with a curse."* The people hearts did not turn back. Immediately after the great tribulation, the Day of the Lord will occur which is Jesus' Second Advent.

In Malachi 3:1 the statement, *"even the messenger of the covenant,"* is referring to Moses. God told Moses to tell the children of Israel about His covenant which He will make with them. God made a covenant with them and promised them a holy nation and a kingdom of priests (Exodus 19:3-6; Deuteronomy 14:2, 16:18-19). God instructed Moses to place the Law written on tablets of stone (The Ten Commandment), Aaron's rod that budded, and an omer of manna in the ark of the covenant or testimony (1st Kings 8:9; Deuteronomy 31:24-26; Exodus 16:31-35; and Numbers 17:10). The *"whom ye delight"* also refers to Moses because the Pharisees and scribes were always reminding Jesus about the Law which Moses gave them.

Chapter Eleven

There are those who say that Moses could not be one of the witnesses because the scripture states that he died and was buried and that Michael, the archangel, contended with the devil about the body of Moses saying, *"The Lord rebuke thee"* (Jude 1:9). Let us remember that Christ is also The Resurrection as well as The Life (John 11:25-26). I am not saying that Moses was resurrected. I am saying that the God we serve is Sovereign, Almighty, and Omnipotent. His ways are not our ways and His thoughts are not our thoughts (Isaiah 55:8-9).

Some believe that these two witnesses are Elijah and Enoch because they were both raptured or caught up and have not died. This statement is assuming that they must return to earth and die before they can spend eternity with the Lord. Remember that to be raptured is to be changed (transformed) in a moment in the twinkling of an eye which is the case for Elijah and Enoch. When Elijah and Enoch were raptured, they would have received some type of spiritual body at that time. Before Jesus incarnation or birth, He had a body that allowed Him to eat and drink in the Old Testament as the Angel of the Lord and Melchizedek, the King of Salem.

While in the earth as Jesus, the Son of Man and the Son of God, He was able to transfigure His mortal physical body to a heavenly body (transfigured) and back to a mortal body (allowing Him to taste death for all men). I believe that will be the case for Elijah and Moses. Their current heavenly bodies (whatever they

Chapter Eleven

are) will be transfigured back to a mortal body (allowing them to taste death). After three and a half days, the Spirit of Life from God will enter into them and they will stand upon their feet. Paul tells us that the 1st Adam was earthly and the last Adam, Jesus, was heavenly and a Life-Giving Spirit (1st Corinthians 15:45-49). They will not enter into the earth via the womb of a woman again. God will send them. How? I do not know. What I do know is that He is the source of all Life in which everything exists. He is the Life and the Resurrection just like He said in the scriptures.

Some Old Testament saints, resurrected at Jesus' resurrection, received their glorified bodies (Matthew 27:50-53; Ephesians 4:8-10; Psalm 68:18-22). At the future rapture (catching away of the church saints), the **<u>dead in Christ</u>** shall rise first and then they which are **<u>alive and remain</u>** shall be caught up together with them in the clouds to meet the Lord in the air and so shall we ever be with the Lord (1st Thessalonians 4:16-17). These raptured saints will receive their glorified bodies at that time and will not have to return to the earth to die. The bible tells us that to be absent from the body is to be present with the Lord (2nd Corinthians 5:8). Flesh and blood cannot inherit the kingdom of God. First Corinthians 15:50-57 says, *"Now this I say, brethren, that flesh and blood cannot inherit the kingdom of God; neither doth corruption inherit incorruption. Behold, I shew you a mystery; We shall not all sleep, but we shall all be changed, in a moment, in the twinkling of an eye, at the last trump: for the trumpet shall sound, and the dead shall be raised incorruptible, and we shall be* *changed. For this corruptible must put on incorruption, and this mortal must put on immortality. So when this corruptible shall have put on incorruption, and this mortal shall have put on immortality, then shall be brought to pass the saying that is written, Death is swallowed up in victory. O death, where is thy sting? O grave, where is thy victory? The sting of death is sin; and the strength of sin is the law. But thanks be to God, which giveth us the victory through our Lord Jesus Christ."* The scripture says that there will be some that will not taste death at His Second Coming (Matthew 16:28; Luke 9:27). The book of 1st Samuel the 2nd chapter says it best, *"<u>The Lord killeth, and maketh alive</u>: He bringeth down to the grave, and bringeth up. The Lord maketh poor, and maketh rich: He bringeth low, and lifteth up. He raiseth up the poor out of the dust, and lifteth up the beggar from the dunghill, to set them among princes, and to make them inherit the throne of glory: for the pillars of the earth are the Lord's, and He hath set the world upon them."*

How can all of this be possible? Just like in Ezekiel, the 37th chapter, the dry bones were revived. Our bones will come together and put on sinews, flesh, and skin at His shout. Our physical body will be raised glorified and will unite with our spiritual body (soul and spirit), without blood, when the Lord Himself shall descend from heaven with a shout, with the voice of the archangel, and with the trump of God (1st Thessalonians 4). They will be just like Jesus' body was at His resurrection (Luke 24:37-43). In 1st John 3:2, *"Beloved, now are we the sons of God, and it doth not yet*

Chapter Eleven

appear what we shall be: but we know that, when He shall appear, we shall be like Him; for we shall see Him as He is." Then we shall be forever and ever with the Lord (John 14:1-3).

7th Trumpet

After the second woe which is the sixth trumpet is passed, the third woe or seventh trumpet comes quickly. Just like the 6th and 7th seal occur quickly together in succession so does the 6th and 7th trumpet occurs quickly in succession.

Moses and Elijah have been killed, revived, resurrected, and ascended. When the seventh angel sounds the seventh trumpet, great voices in heaven rejoices by saying, *"The kingdoms of this world are become the kingdoms of our Lord and of His Christ; and He shall reign for ever and ever."* The twenty-four elders, which sat before God on their seats, fall upon their faces and worship God saying *"We give Thee thanks, O Lord God Almighty, which <u>is</u>, and <u>was</u>, and <u>is to come</u> because Thou hast taken to Thee Thy great power and has reigned. The nations were angry and Thy <u>wrath is come</u> and the time of the dead, that they should be judged, and that Thou should give reward unto thy servants the prophets, and to the saints, and them that fear Thy name, small and great; and should destroy them which destroy the earth."*

It is at the blowing of the seventh trumpet that the rapture of the church occurs. In Revelation 10:6-7, it says that when the seventh angel sounds there should be time no longer and the mystery of God should be finished as He has declared to His servants the prophets. It is at this time that the Lord shall descend from heaven with a shout, with the voice of the archangel, and with the trump of God: and the dead in Christ shall rise first. First Thessalonians 4:13-17 says, *"But I do not want you to be ignorant, brethren, concerning those who have fallen asleep, lest you sorrow as others who have no hope. For if we believe that Jesus died and rose again, even so God will bring with Him those who sleep in Jesus. For this we say to you by the word of the Lord, that we who are alive and remain until the coming of the Lord will by no means precede those who are asleep. For the Lord Himself will descend from heaven with a shout, with the voice of an archangel, and with the trumpet of God. And the dead in Christ will rise first. Then we who are alive and remain shall be caught up together with them in the clouds to meet the Lord in the air. And thus we shall always be with the Lord."*

Just as the heavens opened for Stephen and he could see the Glory of God and Jesus standing at the right hand of God the Father, so will heavens open wide to receive the dead in Christ and those that are alive and remain (Acts 7:55-56). Again, all of this will occur in a moment, in the twinkling of an eye, at the last trump: for the trumpet shall sound, and the dead shall be raised incorruptible, and we shall be changed. For this corruptible must put on incorruption, and this mortal

Chapter Eleven

must put on immortality (1st Corinthians 15:51-52). This is the third woe.

How are the dead raised up? With what type of body do they come? We know when a person dies, the body of the dead returns to dust. If that person died in Christ, their soul and spirit go to be with the Lord (Christ) in Glory waiting for the bodily resurrection to everlasting life. If that person rejected Christ (the unbeliever), their soul and spirit go to Hell just like the rich man in Luke chapter 16 waiting resurrection to everlasting contempt. The bible does not elaborate on the type of body the resurrected unbeliever will have at the Great White Throne Judgment. All we know is that there will be a resurrection of the just and unjust (Acts 24:15; Daniel 12:2). When the believers (just) are resurrected, their body, soul, and spirit will be united just like what happened in Ezekiel 37:5-6. The Lord God will speak to their bones and will cause sinews, flesh, and skin to reunite with their breath (spirit). The resurrected believer shall live in their glorified bodies with the Lord forever. These glorified bodies are flesh and bones that can be handled (touched) and can even eat food. They will be just like Jesus' body in Luke 24:37-43.

It is at this time that the Lord will give white robes to all of His raptured tribulation (not referring to the great tribulation but the current church age) servants the prophets, the saints, and them that fear His name, small and great, at the blowing of the seventh (last) trumpet.

The nations were angry because the wrath of God is come (Psalm 2). The church has been raptured. The time for the great tribulation has come for God to take vengeance on His adversaries for He has reserved His wrath for His enemies (Nahum 1:2). God has not appointed the church to endure His wrath according to 1st Thessalonians 1:10 which says, *"And to wait for His Son from heaven, Whom He raised from the dead, even Jesus, which delivered us from the wrath to come."* and in 1st Thessalonians 5:9-11 which says, *"For God hath not appointed us to wrath, but to obtain salvation by our Lord Jesus Christ, Who died for us, that, whether we wake or sleep, we should live together with Him. Wherefore comfort yourselves together, and edify one another, even as also ye do."* The great tribulation period will last for 3 ½ years and is the time of the pouring out of the 7 vials or bowls judgments.

After the great tribulation period, the great tribulation saints will be raptured the same way or manner as the tribulation saints were at the sound of the seventh trumpet. These shall awake to everlasting life (the believer in Christ – the just or justified). The Lord will give white robes to all of His raptured great tribulation saints who did not worship the Antichrist, his image, nor did they take the mark of the beast. Now, all of the church (tribulation and great tribulation saint) have been raptured. The nation of Israel is

Chapter Eleven

rejoicing by saying the words spoken by Jesus in Luke 13:35, *"Blessed is He that cometh in the name of the Lord."*

The time of the dead that they should be judged has come. The time of the dead refers to them that sleep in the dust of the earth that rejected Christ to be judged. They will be judged after the Great Tribulation, the Second Advent/Coming of Jesus, and the Millennium.

At Jesus' Second Advent, all believers in Christ will receive their rewards or crowns. He will give rewards to His servants the prophets, the saints, and those who fear His name, small and great (Revelation 11:18, 20:4-5, 22:12; Daniel 7:22). This judgment is for rewards and not for sin. There is no condemnation to them in Christ Jesus (Romans 8:1-2). Sin was judged at Calvary with Jesus' death, burial and resurrection which justified the sinner as if they never sinned. Romans 8:3 says, *"For what the law could not do, in that it was weak through the flesh, God sending His Own Son in the likeness of sinful flesh, and for sin, condemned sin in the flesh."* It is At Jesus' Second Advent that He will destroy them which destroy the earth (all of His enemies - the destroyers). Jesus will reign as King for a thousand years in the Millennium. All of those who rejected Christ offer of salvation will be judged along with the rest of the dead after the Millennium at the Great White Throne judgment. They will be awakened to shame and everlasting contempt (the unbelievers – the unjust) (Daniel 12:2). Then, they will be cast into the lake of fire (the second death) where Satan, the Antichrist, the False Prophet were cast and will be tormented day and night forever and ever.

Malachi 3:1, *"Behold, I will send my messenger, and he shall prepare the way before Me: and <u>the Lord, whom ye seek, shall suddenly come to His temple</u>, even the messenger of the covenant, whom ye delight in: behold, he shall come, saith the Lord of hosts."*

The temple of God will be opened in heaven and there was seen in His temple the ark of His covenant (Son of God/Son of Man) representing the Manifested Presence of God. Elijah came first three and a half years earlier before the Great Tribulation. This event occurs at His Second Advent or Coming. There will be lightning, voices, thundering, an earthquake, and great hail just like it was when the Holy Spirit was poured into the earth (Revelation chapter 8; 16:21; Acts 2; Joel chapters 2 & 3). He will come as the later and former rain. Hosea 6:1-3 says, *"Come, and let us return unto the Lord: for He hath torn, and He will heal us; He hath smitten, and He will bind us up. After two days will He revive us: in the third day He will raise us up, and we shall live in His sight. Then shall we know, if we follow on to know the Lord: His going forth is prepared as the morning; and He shall come unto us as the rain, as the latter and former rain unto the earth."*

CHAPTER TWELVE

Woman and the Dragon

There appeared a great wonder in heaven and it is a woman clothed with the sun and the moon under her feet and upon her head a crown of twelve stars. This woman is Mary representing the nation of Israel and the twelve stars are the twelve sons of Jacob (Joshua 7:10-11). Genesis 37:9-10 says, *"And he dreamed yet another dream, and told it his brethren, and said, Behold, I have dreamed a dream more; and, behold, the sun and the moon and the eleven stars made obeisance to me. And he told it to his father, and to his brethren: and his father rebuked him, and said unto him, What is this dream that thou hast dreamed? Shall I and thy mother and thy brethren indeed come to bow down ourselves to thee to the earth?"*

Chapter Twelve

The woman, being with child, is travailing in birth pains as she gives birth to the Messiah. Paul tells us in Romans 9:5, *"Whose are the fathers, and of whom as concerning the flesh Christ came, who is over all, God blessed for ever. Amen."* Jesus, the Christ, is a natural descendant of the fathers or patriarchs (Abraham, Isaac, and Jacob) from the nation of Israel. God tells Satan about this woman in Jeremiah 4:30-31, *"And when thou art spoiled, what wilt thou do? Though thou clothest thyself with crimson, though thou deckest thee with ornaments of gold, though thou rentest thy face with painting, in vain shalt thou make thyself fair; thy lovers will despise thee, they will seek thy life. For I have heard a voice <u>as of a woman</u> in travail, and the anguish as of her that bringeth forth her first child, the voice of the daughter of Zion, that bewaileth herself, that spreadeth her hands, saying, Woe is me now! for my soul is wearied because of murderers."*

There appeared another wonder in heaven of a great red dragon having seven heads, ten horns, and seven crowns upon his heads. This red dragon is Satan, the serpent of old. He will have authority over all nations (seven heads/mountains or continents) and the ten horns are the ten kings that will appear during the great tribulation also known as the time of Jacob's trouble. The seven crowns upon the seven heads mean that he is the king over all the nations and the children of pride (Job 41:34; Ephesians 2:2). He is the leviathan of old. He is actually called the god (prince or ruler) of this world (John 12:31). He is the king of the kingdoms of this world which are represented as the seven

Chapter Twelve

heads/continents in which he has authority over (Revelation 11:15). In the book of Matthew 4:8-10, the scripture confirms his kingship by saying, *"Again, the devil taketh Him up into an exceeding high mountain, and sheweth Him all the kingdoms of the world, and the glory of them; And saith unto Him, All these things will I give thee, if Thou wilt fall down and worship me. Then saith Jesus unto him, Get thee hence, Satan: for it is written, Thou shalt worship the Lord thy God, and Him only shalt thou serve."* He will be the influencing power of the Antichrist and the False Prophet. With his tail, he drew a third part of the stars of heaven and cast them to the earth. The stars of heaven are fallen angels (demonic) and they fell with Satan.

The dragon stood before the woman (the nation of Israel) who was ready to deliver and to devour her child as soon as He was born. This woman (the nation of Israel) is also mentioned in Micah 4:10-11, *"Be in pain, and labour to bring forth, O daughter of Zion, like a woman in travail: for now shalt thou go forth out of the city, and thou shalt dwell in the field, and thou shalt go even to Babylon; there shalt thou be delivered; there the Lord shall redeem thee from the hand of thine enemies. Now also many nations are gathered against thee, that say, Let her be defiled, and let our eye look upon Zion."* The nation of Israel did give birth to the Messiah via the virgin, Mary. Herod, influenced by Satan, wanted to kill the child, Jesus. Joseph being warned by God in a dream had to flee to Egypt with Mary and the baby Jesus (Matthew 2:1-16). Jesus, the Christ, the Son of God and the Son of Man, was born

Chapter Twelve

and is a descendant of the nation of Israel. It was prophesied that He will rule the nations with a rod of iron in which He will do at His Second Coming during His Millennial (one thousand years) reign (Revelation 2:26-27; 20:1-7). During His First Advent or Coming, Jesus was crucified on a Roman's cross thirty-three years later for our sins according to the scripture. He was buried and rose on the third day according to the scriptures (1st Corinthians 15:3-4). He was caught up to God and is seated on His throne at the right hand of God the Father. Acts 1:9-11 says, *"And when He had spoken these things, while they beheld, He was taken up; and a cloud received Him out of their sight. And while they looked stedfastly toward heaven as He went up, behold, two men stood by them in white apparel; Which also said, Ye men of Galilee, why stand ye gazing up into heaven? this same Jesus, which is taken up from you into heaven, shall so come in like manner as ye have seen Him go into heaven."* First Peter 3:22 says, *"Who is gone into heaven, and is on the right hand of God; angels and authorities and powers being made subject unto Him."*

The woman fled into the wilderness where she has a place prepared of God and they should feed her there for one thousand two hundred and sixty days. Jesus said in the gospels, *"When ye therefore shall see the abomination of desolation, spoken of by Daniel the prophet, stand in the holy place, (whoso readeth, let him understand:) Then let them which be in Judaea flee into the mountains: Let him which is on the housetop not come down to take any thing out of his house: Neither let him which is in the field return back to take his clothes."*

Chapter Twelve

And woe unto them that are with child, and to them that give suck in those days! But pray ye that your flight be not in the winter, neither on the Sabbath day: For then shall be great tribulation, such as was not since the beginning of the world to this time, no, nor ever shall be. And except those days should be shortened, there should no flesh be saved: but for the elect's sake those days shall be shortened" (Matthew 24:15-22; Mark 13:14-20; Luke 21:20-22). This time period is called the great tribulation or the time of Jacob's trouble and will be a time of persecution as never before (Jeremiah 30:7). Micah 4:10-11, *"Be in pain, and labour to bring forth, O daughter of Zion, like a woman in travail: for now shalt thou go forth out of the city, and thou shalt dwell in the field, and thou shalt go even to Babylon; there shalt thou be delivered; there the Lord shall redeem thee from the hand of thine enemies. Now also many nations are gathered against thee, that say, Let her be defiled, and let our eye look upon Zion."* In the last days, she will flee into the wilderness, dwell in fields, and eventually to Mystery Babylon which is New York City located in the United States of America. At the end of the great tribulation, the Lord Himself will deliver her from all of her enemies and return her to her land.

There was a war in heaven. Michael and his angels fought against the dragon (Satan). Satan and his angels fought back. Satan and his angels did not prevail and there was found no place anymore in heaven for them. The great dragon was cast out, that old serpent, called the Devil, and Satan, who deceives the whole world. He was cast out into the earth and his angels were cast out

Chapter Twelve

with him. Jesus said in John 12:31-33, *"Now is the judgment of this world: now shall <u>the prince of this world be cast out.</u> And I, if I be lifted up from the earth, will draw all men unto Me. This He said, signifying what death He should die."* The prince of this world is Satan.

Then John hears a loud voice saying in heaven, *"Now is come salvation, and strength, and the kingdom of our God, and the power of His Christ: for the accuser of our brethren is cast down, which accused them before our God day and night. And they overcame him by the blood of the Lamb, and by the word of their testimony; and they loved not their lives unto the death. Therefore rejoice, ye heavens, and ye that dwell in them. Woe to the inhabiters of the earth and of the sea! for the devil is come down unto you, having great wrath, because he knoweth that he hath but a short time."* When the dragon saw that he was cast to the earth, he persecuted the woman which brought forth the man child. The woman was given two wings of a great eagle so that she might fly into the wilderness, into her place, where she is nourished for a time, and times, and half a time (3 ½ years), from the face of the serpent. Satan will persecute the woman, the nation of Israel, during the great tribulation for three and one-half years. Israel will be surrounded by her enemies and will have to flee into the wilderness or mountains. She will be protected by the Lord and by those that know their God who will be strong and take action (Daniel 11:32). In Daniel chapter 7, the eagle with two wings that helps Israel during the Great Tribulation represents the United States of America

Chapter Twelve

along with the United Nations Security Council located in The Headquarters of the United Nations.

The serpent cast out of his mouth water as a flood after the woman so that he might cause her to be carried away by the flood. There will be a flood of persecution as never before. Her enemies will be compassed around her. The scripture states that when the enemy shall come in like a flood, the Spirit of the Lord shall lift up a standard against him (Isaiah 59:19).

The earth will help the woman. The earth is referring to the dry land masses or the seven continents (heads) which are figurative of all nations united as one (Genesis 1:10; Revelation 17:9). The earth opened her mouth and swallowed up the flood which the dragon cast out of his mouth. The Headquarters of the United Nations located in New York City in the United States of America will help the woman for three and one-half years. Again, the earth is figurative of the seven heads which represent the seven mountains, continents, or the entire world in which the whore (Mystery Babylon) sits and has control over (Revelation 17:9).

Satan was angry with the woman and went to make war with the remnant of her seed which is the church consisting of both of believing Jew and Gentile believers who keep the commandments of God and have the testimony of Jesus Christ. Not only will the nation of Israel be persecuted during the great tribulation, but the 144,000 believing Jews will be persecuted along with the Gentile Christian believers who will come to faith in Jesus, after the rapture of the church. Those that will

Chapter Twelve

not receive the mark of the beast nor worship the Antichrist or his image will be martyred for their witness of Jesus and for the word of God (Revelation 20:4).

CHAPTER THIRTEEN

The First Beast out of the Sea (The Antichrist)

John, standing on the sand by the sea, sees a beast rise out of the sea having seven heads and ten horns. Upon his horns were ten crowns and upon his heads were the name of blasphemy. In chapter 12, we are told that Satan has authority over the seven heads (mountains or continents) because upon the seven heads were crowns. Satan is the god (prince or ruler) of this world (John 12:31). Ephesians 2:2-3 says, *"Wherein in time past ye walked according to the course of this world, according to the prince of the power of the air, the spirit that now worketh in the children of disobedience: Among whom also we all had our conversation in times past in the lusts of our flesh, fulfilling the desires of the flesh and of the mind; and were by nature the children of wrath, even as others."*

Chapter Thirteen

The beast mentioned in this chapter is the Antichrist. When the Antichrist rises up, his seven heads are not crowned which means that he has no authority at first over the entire world but will receive authority from Satan. The seven mountains/continents (nations – entire world) are blasphemous representing the kingdoms of this world called the children of disobedience. This statement shows us the state of the nations/world during the great tribulation. Remember the first three and a half years of the Antichrist's reign he will be a man of peace. The ten kings mentioned have been given authority because they are crowned. The Antichrist will rise up and rule over all nations during the great tribulation. The seven heads are the nations or continents that he will rule over. The ten horns are the ten future kings that will eventually give their power to the Antichrist. The nations (children of disobedience/wrathful) will be full of blasphemy because they will worship the Antichrist, his image, and receive the mark of the beast.

The dragon (Satan) gave him (the Antichrist) his power, his seat, and his great authority. In Luke 4:5-8, *"And the devil, taking Him up into an high mountain, shewed unto Him all the kingdoms of the world in a moment of time. And the devil said unto Him, All this power will I give Thee, and the glory of them: for that is delivered unto me; and to whomsoever I will I give it. If Thou therefore wilt worship me, all shall be Thine. And Jesus answered and said unto him, Get thee behind Me, Satan: for it is written, Thou shalt worship the Lord thy God, and Him only shalt thou serve."* Remember Satan is the king of the kingdoms of this world which are the seven heads (the nations) which he has authority over.

Chapter Thirteen

The beast was like a leopard and his feet were as the feet of a bear and his mouth of a lion is the Antichrist. This beast is mentioned in Daniel Chapter 7, verses 4-6 as the third beast.

Daniel 7– Three Beasts

"Daniel spoke, saying, "I saw in my vision by night, and behold, the four winds of heaven were stirring up the Great Sea and four great beasts came up from the sea, each different from the other. The first was like a lion, and had eagle's wings: I beheld till the wings thereof were plucked, and it was lifted up from the earth, and made stand upon the feet as a man, and a man's heart was given to it. And behold another beast, a second, like to a bear, and it raised up itself on one side, and it had three ribs in the mouth of it between the teeth of it: and they said thus unto it, Arise, devour much flesh. After this I beheld, and lo another, like a leopard, which had upon the back of it four wings of a fowl; the beast had also four heads; and dominion was given to it." Daniel 7:2-6

Daniel saw in his vision at night and beheld four winds of heaven stirring up the Great Sea (Mediterranean Sea) and four great beasts came up from the sea, each different from the other. As I was watching one of Irwin Baxter's End of the Age program and he told us the lion is Great Britain. The eagle's wings that were plucked off of the lion and lifted up from the earth and made stand upon his feet as a man with a man's heart is the United States of America. The man and the man's heart represent the governmental body of the United States of America which is called Uncle Sam and I agree.

Chapter Thirteen

The Lord revealed to me that this beast is Mystery Babylon known as New York City. It used to be the capital of The United States of America. If you look on a map at the continent of North America, consisting of Canada, The United States of America, and Mexico, you will see that the continent resemble an eagle coming in for a landing or hunting for a fish. South America looks mostly like the foot of the bear from Alexander the Great Grecian Empire from where some of the ten kings will arise. South America is not the foot of the bear that will attack Mystery Babylon. Could this be what the Lion of Babylon statue in Iraq is depicting? The eagle wings removed from the Lion of Babylon. We know that in one day Mystery Babylon will be destroyed by ten kings (Revelation 16:19-21; 17:12-18).

The Lion of Babylon in Iraq is a statue of a lion with his wings plucked off standing above a man lying down. In Revelation 17, there is a woman, Mystery Babylon, riding on a beast that is called the Antichrist. These ten kings will come from the old Babylonian Empire that was conquered by the Medes and Persians Empire then later conquered by the Grecian Empire. God revealed to Nebuchadnezzar what would happen to his Babylonian Empire (Daniel 2). These ten kings that are currently a member of The Headquarters of the United Nations, a united one worldwide governing body, located in The United States of America (the eagle). They will unite as the Lion of Babylon and destroy New York City, the original capital city or governing body of The United States of America (the man – Uncle Sam). Remember that The Headquarters of the United Nations and its United Nations Security Council are not a part of The United States of America. They are located in New York City. The Lion of Babylon is a man-made symbol just like the ball drop on New Year's

Chapter Thirteen

Eve in Times Square, New York City. *(See Revelation The 16th Chapter – The 7th Vial.)*

On the same Irwin Baxter's End of the Age program, he tells us that the bear is Russia that rises up on one side and I agree. In Ezekiel the 38th and 39th chapters, Ezekiel is told by the Sovereign Lord to prophesy against Gog, of the land of Magog, the prince of Rosh, Meshech, and Tubal. Rosh is modern day Russia. Before and after the Millennium, they will be defeated by the Jesus, the Word of God or the Ancient of Days, in Jerusalem.

Russia has two sides because it sits on two continents. If you look at Russia on a map, you will see that the country resembles a bear lying down on one side. The three ribs in the mouth of the bear and between his teeth said to the bear, *"Arise, devour much flesh"* is Satan (the Dragon), the Antichrist, and the False Prophet. The three ribs mean three persons. When the sixth vial is poured out, these three unclean spirits like frogs will come out of the mouth of the dragon (Satan), the beast (Antichrist), and the false prophet. They are the spirits of devils working miracles which go forth to the kings of the earth and the whole world to gather them to the battle of that great day (Second Advent or Coming of Jesus) (Revelation 16:13-14). The bear rising up on one side is figuratively speaking of his bow in his left hand and arrows in his right hand and his readiness to strike his enemies (Ezekiel 39:3).

This leopard represents the Antichrist (a future fallen pope) according to Revelation the 13th chapter. This is the old Grecian Empire ruled by Alexander the Great in which Antiochus IV Epiphanes, a type of antichrist, emerged. The Antichrist, a future fallen

Chapter Thirteen

pope, will have the same characteristics and traits as Antiochus IV Epiphanes. He will be blasphemous and do some of the same things as Antiochus IV Epiphanes. If you look at the old Grecian Empire on a map, it will reveal the mouth of a lion and the feet of a bear. There are at least ten countries currently that are included in this empire. It is from this empire, I believe, that the ten kings will emerge and give their power to the Antichrist. The leopard had upon his back four wings of a fowl. A turkey is a fowl and represents the country of Turkey. The four wings mean that the country of Turkey sits on two continents, Europe and Asia. The four heads represent the four continents or large land masses surrounded by water on three sides. The Antichrist will have dominion given to him, by the ten kings, to rule over this region. I believe that the four heads are Europe, Asia, Africa, and Saudi Arabia since they are all included in this empire. I know that Saudi Arabia is not a continent but it is surrounded by water on three of its sides. The beast that Mystery Babylon sits upon is the Antichrist (Revelation 17:3, 8).

Each of these kingdoms is diverse from one another. The first is a city (Mystery Babylon – New York City), the second is a country or nation (Russia), the third is an individual (the Antichrist – a future fallen pope), and the fourth is a one worldwide governing body (The Headquarters of the United Nations – United Nations Security Council). These are all end time players during the great tribulation or the last 3 ½ years of the week of Daniel.

Back to the text…

Satan will give the Antichrist his power, his position, and his great authority. On one of his heads or

Chapter Thirteen

continents that he has dominion over, he will receive a deadly wound and be healed. The entire world will wonder after the Antichrist. Possibly, one of his allies or nations that he rules over will be attacked, but not completely destroyed and will recover. The nations will worship the dragon (Satan) and the beast (Antichrist) and say, *"Who is like unto the beast? Who is able to make war with him?"* There was given to him a mouth speaking great things and blasphemies. Power was given to him to continue for forty-two months. These forty-two months are the last three and a half years of the Antichrist's reign called the great tribulation. Matthew 24:21-22 says, *"For then shall be great tribulation, such as was not since the beginning of the world to this time, no, nor ever shall be. And except those days should be shortened, there should no flesh be saved: but for the elect's sake those days shall be shortened."* The Antichrist will reign for seven years (days) which is called the week of Daniel (Daniel 9:7). In the middle of his reign, he will break his seven-year covenant agreement. He will open his mouth to blaspheme against God, God's Name, God's tabernacle, and them that dwell in heaven. It was given to him to make war with the saints and to overcome them. Power was given to him over all kindreds, tongues, and nations. Daniel 11:41 says, *"He shall enter also into the glorious land, and many countries shall be overthrown: but these shall escape out of his hand, even Edom, and Moab, and the chief of the children of Ammon."* The glorious land is Israel. All that dwell upon the earth shall worship him whose names are not written in the book of life of the Lamb slain from the foundation of the world. In order for the entire world to worship the Antichrist, lets us know that the church has been caught up (raptured) prior to the great tribulation.

Chapter Thirteen

If any man has an ear, let him hear. *"He that leadeth into captivity shall go into captivity: he that killeth with the sword must be killed with the sword."* Here is the patience (perseverance) and the faith of the saints. Satan will one day be chained in a pit for a thousand years with a final destination of the Lake of Fire where he will be joining the Antichrist and the False Prophet, who proceeded him (Revelation 19:20; 20:1-6, 10).

The Second Beast out of the Earth (False Prophet)

Johns sees another beast coming up out of the earth and he had two horns like a lamb and speaks like a dragon is the False Prophet. He exercises all the power of the first beast and causes them that dwell in the earth to worship the Antichrist whose deadly wound was healed. Remember that the deadly wound on the Antichrist head refers to the fact that the Antichrist will be hit on one of his ruling continents (heads) and recover. The false prophet will do great sign and wonders and even makes fire come down from heaven on the earth in the sight of men. He will deceive them by the means of those miracles which he had the power to do in the sight of the beast (Antichrist). He will say to those that dwell on the earth that they should make an image to the beast which was wounded by a sword and lived. He will give life to the image of the beast and cause the image to speak. He will cause those that will not worship the image of the beast to be killed.

The Mark of the Beast

He will cause all, both small and great, rich and poor, free and bond, to receive a mark in their right hand or in their foreheads. No man will be able to buy or sell except they have the mark, the name of the beast, or the number of his name. In this chapter, *"Here is wisdom. Let him that hath understanding count the number of the beast: for it is the number of a man; and his number is six hundred threescore and six."*

I personally believe that the mark of the beast is some kind of mind control technology that affects the person mental lobe of the brain. It is Satan using mankind to enter into the mind of another man's thought process by controlling his thoughts (forehead) and behavior (works – the hand). As we know, God never intended for man to dwell within another man's mind and control his thoughts and behavior. It is with the mind that we serve the Lord. First Chronicles 28:9 says, *"And thou, Solomon my son, know thou the God of thy father, and serve Him with a perfect heart and with a willing mind: for the Lord searcheth all hearts, and understandeth all the imaginations of the thoughts: if thou seek Him, He will be found of thee; but if thou forsake Him, He will cast thee off for ever."* Only the Holy Ghost is sent to indwell man and influence his thoughts and behavior. The difference between the two is that one can be with or without the man's consent or permission and the Holy Ghost is always with your permission and agreement. Mind Control technology is satanic and the Holy Ghost indwelling is of God and holy. He gives you "the will" and "the want to do" the will of God. Philippians 2:13 says, *"For it is God which worketh in you both to will and to do of His good pleasure."* Mind Control technology can be very detrimental if gets into the wrong persons hands.

The human brain is divided into several parts. The frontal lobe of the brain controls the following:

Frontal lobe

Chapter Thirteen

- Personality, behavior, emotions
- Judgment, planning, problem solving
- Speech: speaking and writing (Broca's area)
- Body movement (motor strip)
- Intelligence, concentration, self-awareness

Source: The Mayfield Clinic

(https://www.mayfieldclinic.com/PE-natBrain.htm)

Satellites and Global Positioning Systems (GPS) - Flying Scroll

Another form of technology that is available and that the Antichrist and False Prophet will use is satellites. Satellites and Global Positioning Systems (GPS) can observe, talk, locate, and navigate every movement anywhere on or near the earth where there is an unobstructed view or line of sight. Today, a person can purchase a voice-driven, voice-activated, personal assistants technology for our homes. These technologies can be found on our smart cell phones, iPad, laptops, and personal computers. Our vehicles, homes, and smart cell phones can be locked, unlocked and tracked via GPS. Did you know that satellites are mentioned in the bible? Some satellites are being used for good and some for other reasons. They are being used by Christian networks to broadcast the good news of Jesus Christ's birth, death, burial, and resurrection around the world. The scripture says before Christ returns, the gospel of the kingdom must be preached to the entire world for a witness to all nations and then shall the end come (Matthew 24:14).

When we look at pictures of satellites, some of them look like flying scrolls. In Zechariah 5:1-4, the prophet

Chapter Thirteen

of God has a vision in which he sees a flying scroll. Zechariah says, *"Then I turned, and lifted up mine eyes, and looked, and behold a flying roll. And he said unto me, What seest thou? And I answered, I see a flying roll; the length thereof is twenty cubits, and the breadth thereof ten cubits. Then said he unto me, This is the curse that goeth forth over the face of the whole earth: for every one that <u>stealeth</u> (thief) shall be cut off as <u>on this side</u> according to it; and every one that <u>sweareth (liar)</u> shall be cut off as <u>on that side</u> according to it. I will bring it forth, saith the Lord of hosts, and it shall enter into the house of the thief, and into the house of him that sweareth falsely by my name: and it shall remain in the midst of his house, and shall consume it with the timber thereof and the stones thereof."* Notice that the scroll in Zechariah vision is a double edge sword. Hebrews 4:12-13 says, *"For the word of God is quick, and powerful, and sharper than any two edged sword, piercing even to the dividing asunder of soul and spirit, and of the joints and marrow, and is a discerner of the thoughts and intents of the heart. Neither is there <u>any creature</u> that is not manifest in His sight: but all things are <u>naked and opened</u> unto the eyes of Him with Whom we have to do."*

This scroll is symbolic of the law (The Ten Commandments). Notice that the scripture in Zechariah mentions two of The Ten Commandments. Thou shalt not steal and thou shalt not bear false witness. We would not have known sin if there was no law. If there is no law, then there could be no transgression against the law. Is the law evil? Absolutely not. Romans 7:7-8, says it best, *"What shall we say then? Is the law sin? God forbid. Nay, I had not known sin, but by the law: for I had not known lust, except the law had said, Thou shalt not covet. But sin, taking occasion by the commandment, wrought in me all*

Chapter Thirteen

manner of concupiscence (strong desire). For without the law sin was dead." First Corinthians 15:56 says that, *"The sting of death is sin; and the strength of sin is the law."*

The law, which is holy, is what Satan uses to accuse mankind day and night before God, other men, and ourselves. John chapter 8:3-11 says, *"And the scribes and Pharisees brought unto Him a woman taken in adultery; and when they had set her in the midst, They say unto Him, Master, this woman was taken in adultery, in the very act. Now Moses in the law commanded us, that such should be stoned: but what sayest Thou? This they said, tempting Him, that they might have to accuse Him. But Jesus stooped down, and with His finger wrote on the ground, as though He heard them not. So when they continued asking Him, He lifted up Himself, and said unto them, He that is without sin among you, let him first cast a stone at her. And again He stooped down, and wrote on the ground. And they which heard it, being convicted by their own conscience, went out one by one, beginning at the eldest, even unto the last: and Jesus was left alone, and the woman standing in the midst. When Jesus had lifted up Himself, and saw none but the woman, He said unto her, Woman, where are those thine accusers? hath no man condemned thee? She said, No man, Lord. And Jesus said unto her, Neither do I condemn thee: go, and sin no more."* When the woman, caught in adultery, was brought before Jesus, the scribes and Pharisees accused her to Jesus using the law as their basis for the accusation. Jesus said to the scribes and Pharisees that *"He that is without sin among you, let him first cast a stone at her."* Notice that each time an accusation was made that Jesus stooped down and wrote with His finger on the ground. He is letting us know that transgression against the Ten

Chapter Thirteen

Commandment (or the Law) written on tablets of stone with the finger of God is what is actually accusing the woman and them (Exodus 31:18). By Jesus' death on the cross and resurrection, He took the Law away. Therefore, Christ is the end of the law for righteousness to everyone that believes (Romans 10:4).

The Ten Commandments were given to the Israelites by God via Moses in the wilderness and not to the Gentiles (Exodus 31:18). *"Therefore by the <u>deeds of the law</u> there shall no flesh be justified in His sight: for by the law is the knowledge of sin"* (Romans 3:20). However, there is hope for all mankind according to Galatians 3:10-14, *"For as many as are of the <u>works of the law</u> are under the curse: for it is written, Cursed is every one that continueth not in all things which are written in the book of the law to do them. But that no man is justified by the law in the sight of God, it is evident: for, The just shall live by faith. And the law is not of faith: but, The man that doeth them shall live in them. Christ hath redeemed us from the curse of the law, being made a curse for us: for it is written, Cursed is every one that hangeth on a tree: That the blessing of Abraham might come on the Gentiles through Jesus Christ; that we might receive the promise of the Spirit through faith."*

Jesus Christ, Who knew no sin, became sin and nailed sin to the cross (2nd Corinthians 2:21). He nailed the curse of the law which is the Word of God (Jesus the Christ being made sin – a curse for us) to the cross because of our transgressions. Colossians 2:12-15 says, *"Buried with Him in baptism, wherein also ye are risen with Him through the faith of the operation of God, Who hath raised Him from the dead. And you, being dead in your sins and the uncircumcision of your flesh, hath He*

Chapter Thirteen

quickened together with Him, having forgiven you all trespasses; <u>Blotting out the handwriting of ordinances that was against us, which was contrary to us, and took it out of the way, nailing it to His cross</u>; And having spoiled principalities and powers, He made a shew of them openly, triumphing over them in it." Just like the ram on Mount Moriah was caught in the thicket, so was Jesus (Genesis 22:13). No other man could redeem man. He was the only One Who could destroy the curse of the law and the ordinances against us and takes it away. Jesus is our Sacrificial Lamb and our High Priest after the order of Melchizedek, the King of Salem because He is the Ancient of Days (Daniel 7:9-14, 22). He is the only High Priest Who could enter into the tabernacle of God in the third heaven and offer His blood upon the Mercy Seat for our sins and not His Own. He entered into the Holy Place in the third heaven once and for all and obtained eternal redemption for us. *"For Christ is not entered into the Holy Places made with hands, which are the figures of the true; but into heaven itself, now to appear in the presence of God for us: Nor yet that He should offer Himself often, as the High Priest entereth into the Holy Place every year with blood of others"* (Hebrews 9:24-25).

The law is now taken away and we are living in days like the days of Noah, Abraham, and Joseph. Where there is no written law given, there is no transgression against the law. Even though, sin is present. We are now considered blameless as if we never sinned (Philippians 2:15; 1st Corinthians 1:8; 2nd Peter 3:14; 1st Thessalonians 5:23). Because we love Him, we keep ourselves from sinning with the His Help (the Comforter) even though, we are capable of sinning. *"We know that whosoever is born of God sinneth not; but He that is begotten of God keepeth himself, and that*

Chapter Thirteen

wicked one toucheth him not" (1st John 5:18). **The only difference between the patriarchs and us is that the Holy Spirit indwells us and works in us to will and do His good pleasure (Philippians 2:13).** *"Being confident of this very thing, that He which hath begun a good work in you will perform it until the day of Jesus Christ"* **(Philippians 1:6). We are in the dispensation of grace and live according to His Divine Promises (2nd Peter 1:3-4).**

In Galatians 3:6-15 the scripture says, *"Even as Abraham believed God, and it was accounted to him for righteousness. Know ye therefore that they which are of faith, the same are the children of Abraham. And the scripture, foreseeing that God would justify the heathen through faith, preached before the gospel unto Abraham, saying, In thee shall all nations be blessed. So then they which are of faith are blessed with faithful Abraham. For as many as are of the works of the law are under the curse: for it is written, Cursed is every one that continueth not in all things which are written in the book of the law to do them. But that no man is justified by the law in the sight of God, it is evident: for, The just shall live by faith. And the law is not of faith: but, The man that doeth them shall live in them. Christ hath redeemed us from the curse of the law, being made a curse for us: for it is written, Cursed is every one that hangeth on a tree: That the blessing of Abraham might come on the Gentiles through Jesus Christ; that we might receive the promise of the Spirit through faith. Brethren, I speak after the manner of men; Though it be but a man's covenant, yet if it be confirmed, no man disannulleth, or addeth thereto."* **In Abraham days, there was no law to accuse them. Even though, they did sin. Where there is no law, there is no transgression against the law. This is why 1st John 3:3-11 says,** *"And every man that hath this hope in him*

Chapter Thirteen

purifieth himself, even as he is pure. Whosoever committeth sin transgresseth also the law: for sin is the transgression of the law. And ye know that He was manifested to take away our sins; and in Him is no sin. Whosoever abideth in Him sinneth not: whosoever sinneth hath not seen Him, neither known Him. Little children, let no man deceive you: he that doeth righteousness is righteous, even as he is righteous. He that committeth sin is of the devil; for the devil sinneth from the beginning. For this purpose the Son of God was manifested, that He might destroy the works of the devil. Whosoever is born of God doth not commit sin; for His seed remaineth in him: and he cannot sin, because he is born of God. In this the children of God are manifest, and the children of the devil: whosoever doeth not righteousness is not of God, neither he that loveth not his brother. For this is the message that ye heard from the beginning, that we should love one another."

Therefore, being blameless, the scripture in Romans 6:1-2, 12-14, 20-22 says, *"Shall we continue in sin, that grace may abound? God forbid. How shall we, that are dead to sin, live any longer therein?...Let not sin therefore reign in your mortal body, that ye should obey it in the lusts thereof. Neither yield ye your members as instruments of unrighteousness unto sin: but yield yourselves unto God, as those that are alive from the dead, and your members as instruments of righteousness unto God. For sin shall not have dominion over you: for ye are not under the law, but under grace...For when ye were the servants of sin, ye were free from righteousness. What fruit had ye then in those things whereof ye are now ashamed? for the end of those things is death. But now being made free from sin, and become servants to God, ye have your fruit unto holiness, and the end everlasting life."*

Chapter Thirteen

Because the law could not give life eternal nor justify the sinner, we needed a Savior (Galatians 3:21). John 3:15-19 says, *"That whosoever believeth in Him should not perish, but have eternal life. For God so loved the world, that He gave His only begotten Son, that whosoever believeth in Him should not perish, but have everlasting life. For God sent not His Son into the world to condemn the world; but that the world through Him might be saved. He that believeth on Him is not condemned: but he that believeth not is condemned already, because he hath not believed in the name of the only begotten Son of God. And this is the condemnation, that Light is come into the world, and men loved darkness rather than Light, because their deeds were evil."*

And in Romans 8:1-3, *"There is therefore now no condemnation to them which are in Christ Jesus, who walk not after the flesh, but after the Spirit. For the law of the Spirit of life in Christ Jesus hath made me free from the law of sin and death. For what the law could not do, in that it was weak through the flesh, God sending His own Son in the likeness of sinful flesh, and for sin, condemned sin in the flesh."* **We are no longer condemned, but we are justified as if we never sinned. To reject Christ's and His gospel of grace is to deny that Jesus Christ is Lord, Savior, and God. Jesus is the Way, the Truth, and the Life (John 14:6). As long as there is breath in a person's body, salvation is available to them to confess the Lord Jesus and accept Jesus as Savior. The gospel of grace is to believe on the Lord Jesus Christ's death, burial, and resurrection (Romans 10:9-10).**

CHAPTER FOURTEEN

The Lamb of God and the 144,000

John looks and sees the Lamb of God standing on Mount Zion in Jerusalem along with the hundred and forty-four thousand Jewish believers who have their Father's name written in their foreheads. They were sealed (Revelation 7:3-8). Then John hears a voice from heaven as the voice of many waters and as the voice of a great thunder. He also hears the voice of harpers harping with their harps. They sang as it were a new song before the throne and before the four beasts (living creatures) and the (twenty-four) elders. No man could learn that song, but the hundred and forty-four thousand which were redeemed from the earth. These hundred and forty-four thousand were not defiled with women because they are virgins. They follow the Lamb wherever He goes. They were redeemed from among men, being the first fruits to God and the Lamb. In their mouth was found no guile. They are without fault before the throne of God.

Three Angels Warnings of Soon Judgments to Come

John saw another angel fly in the midst of heaven having the everlasting gospel to preach to them that dwell on the earth, to every nation, kindred, tongue, and people, *"Saying with a loud voice, Fear God, and give glory to Him; for the hour of His judgment is come: and worship Him that made heaven, and earth, and the sea, and the fountains of waters."* The first angel having the everlasting gospel to preach is warning them that dwell on the earth to worship God and give Him glory because the hour of His judgment is come. It is written that when the gospel is preached in all the world for a witness to all nations, then shall the end come (Matthew 24:14).

There followed the second angel saying, *"Babylon is fallen, is fallen, that great city, because she made all nations drink of the wine of the wrath of her fornication."* This angel is letting them know that the great city of Mystery Babylon is fallen and not to participate in her sins. God will bring punishment on Mystery Babylon at the seventh vial judgments just before Christ's Second Advent or Coming (Revelation 16:19-21).

Chapter Fourteen

The third angel followed them saying with a loud voice, *"If any man worship the beast and his image, and receive his mark in his forehead, or in his hand, The same shall drink of the wine of the wrath of God, which is poured out without mixture into the cup of His indignation; and he shall be tormented with fire and brimstone in the presence of the holy angels, and in the presence of the Lamb: And the smoke of their torment ascendeth up for ever and ever: and they have no rest day nor night, who worship the beast and his image, and whosoever receiveth the mark of his name."* **This angel is saying that if any man worship the Antichrist, his image, and receive his mark in their forehead or hand shall drink of the wine of the wrath of God. God's wrath will be poured out without mixture means the full strength and not diluted. Those individuals will be tormented with fire and brimstone (the lake of fire) in the presence of the holy angels and in the presence of the Lamb. The smoke of their torment ascends up forever and ever and they will have no rest day or night.**

Here is the patience (perseverance or endurance) of the saints and they that keep the commandments of God and the faith of Jesus. John hears a voice from heaven saying, *"Write, Blessed are the dead which die in the Lord from henceforth: Yea, saith the Spirit, that they may rest from their labours; and their works do follow them."* **He is telling John to write and remind the saints of their blessed hope. In other words, they are to be faithful even to the point of death and to rest in Him because**

their works do follow them. He will not forget their labor of love (1ˢᵗ Thessalonians 1:3; Hebrews 6:10).

Harvesting the Earth at the Second Advent & the Great Winepress

John looked and beheld a white cloud and upon the cloud, One, sat like the Son of Man having on His head a golden crown and in His hand a sharp sickle.

Another angel came out of the temple crying with a loud voice to Him that sat on the cloud, *"Thrust in Thy sickle, and reap: for the time is come for Thee to reap; for the harvest of the earth is ripe."* And He that sat on the cloud thrust in His sickle on the earth and the earth was reaped. This is the harvesting of saints that were saved during the great tribulation and endured.

And another angel came out of the temple which is in heaven, he also having a sharp sickle.

And another angel came out from the altar, which had power over fire; and cried with a loud cry to Him that had the sharp sickle saying, *"Thrust in Thy sharp sickle, and gather the clusters of the vine of the earth; for her grapes are fully ripe."* And the angel thrust in His sickle into the earth and gathered the vine of the earth and cast it into the great winepress of the wrath of God. The winepress was trodden outside the city and blood came out of the winepress to the horse bridles by the space of a thousand and six hundred furlongs (approximately 200 miles). This is the harvesting of those that worshipped the beast, his image, and received the mark of the beast during the great tribulation (Revelation 19:13-21).

Matthew 13:30 says, *"Let both (wheat and tare) grow together until the harvest: and in the time of harvest I will say to the reapers, Gather ye together first the tares, and bind them in bundles to burn them: but gather the wheat into my barn."* **Both of these harvestings occurs at the Second Coming of the Son of Man. Jesus explains this to His disciples in Matthew 13:36-43**.

^{36} "Then Jesus sent the multitude away, and went into the house: and His disciples came unto Him, saying, Declare unto us the parable of the tares of the field.
^{37} He answered and said unto them, He that soweth the good seed is the Son of Man;
^{38} The field is the world; the good seed are the children of the kingdom; but the tares are the children of the wicked one;
^{39} The enemy that sowed them is the devil; the harvest is the end of the world; and the reapers are the angels.
^{40} As therefore the tares are gathered and burned in the fire; so shall it be in the end of this world.
^{41} The Son of Man shall send forth His angels, and they shall gather out of His kingdom all things that offend, and them which do iniquity;
^{42} And shall cast them into a furnace of fire: there shall be wailing and gnashing of teeth.

Chapter Fourteen

^{43} Then shall the righteous shine forth as the sun in the kingdom of their Father. Who hath ears to hear, let him hear."

CHAPTER FIFTEEN

Seven Angels Having The Seven Last Plagues

John sees another great and marvelous sign in the third heaven with seven angels having the last seven plagues because in them is filled up with the wrath of God. Then, he sees a sea of glass mingled with fire and those that had gotten the victory over the Antichrist, his image, his mark, and over the number of his name, stand on the sea of glass, having the harps of God. The sea of glass mingled with fire is the sea reflecting (glass) the fiery throne of God (Daniel 7:9-10). They sing the song of Moses, the servant of God, and the song of the Lamb saying, *"Great and marvelous are Thy works, Lord God Almighty; Just and true are Thy ways, Thou King of saints. Who shall not fear Thee, O Lord, and glorify Thy*

Chapter Fifteen

name? for Thou only art Holy: for all nations shall come and worship before Thee; for Thy judgments are made manifest."

After that, John looks and beheld the temple of the tabernacle of the testimony in heaven was opened. Seven angels came out of the temple, having the seven plagues, clothed in pure and white linen, and having their breasts girded with golden girdles. One of the four beasts gave to the seven angel's seven golden vials full of the wrath of God, Who lives forever and ever. The temple was filled with smoke from the glory of God and from His power; and no man was able to enter into the temple until the seven plagues of the seven angels were fulfilled.

CHAPTER SIXTEEN

The Seven Vials (Is to Come)

These seven vial or bowl judgments occur after the rapture of the church and after the blowing of the seventh trumpet.

John hears a great voice out of the temple saying to the seven angels, *"Go your ways, and pour out the vials of the wrath of God upon the earth."*

1st Vial

The first angel poured his vial upon the earth and there fell a noisome and grievous sore upon the men which had the mark of the beast and upon them which worshipped his image.

Chapter Sixteen

2nd Vial

The second angel poured his vial upon the sea and it became as the blood of a dead man and every living soul died in the sea.

3rd Vial

The third angel poured his vial upon the rivers and fountains of waters and they became blood. Then, John hears the angel in charge of the waters say, *"Thou art righteous, O Lord, which art, and wast, and shalt be, because thou hast judged thus. For they have shed the blood of saints and prophets, and Thou hast given them blood to drink; for they are worthy."* Then, John hears another angel out of the altar say, *"Even so, Lord God Almighty, true and righteous are Thy judgments.*

4th Vial

The fourth angel poured his vial upon the sun and power was given to him to scorch men with fire. The men that were scorched with great heat blasphemed the name of God, Who has power over these plagues, and they did not repent nor give God glory.

5th Vial

The fifth angel poured his vial upon the seat of the beast and his kingdom was full of darkness and they gnawed their tongues for pain and blasphemed the God of heaven because of their pains and their sores. They did not repent of their deeds.

6th Vial

Chapter Sixteen

The sixth angel poured his vial upon the great river Euphrates and the water was dried up so that the way of the kings of the east might be prepared. Then, John sees three unclean spirits (demonic) like frogs come out of the mouth of the dragon (Satan), out of the mouth of the beast (Antichrist), and out of the mouth of the false prophet. These unclean spirits are the spirits of devils, working miracles, which go forth to the kings of the earth and the whole world to gather them to the battle of that great day of God Almighty (Second Advent or Coming). Revelation 16:15 says, *"Behold, I come as a thief. Blessed is he that watcheth, and keepeth his garments, lest he walk naked, and they see his shame."* He gathered them together into a place called in the Hebrew tongue Armageddon.

7th Vial

The seventh angel poured his vial into the air and there came a great voice out of the temple of heaven, from the throne saying, *"It is done."* There were voices, thunders, and lightnings. There was an extremely great and mighty earthquake such as never have been since man has been on the earth.

The great city was divided into three parts. The cities of the nation fell. This great city is New York City (USA) which is currently divided into three major sections. It is where The Headquarters of the United Nations resides in the Manhattan Borough. One section consists of Staten Island, another section consists of Manhattan and The Bronx, and the third section consists of Brooklyn and Queens. Great Babylon (New York City) came in remembrance before God to give to her the cup of the wine of the fierceness of His wrath. Every island fled away and the mountains were not found (Revelation 18:21-23). I believe that there will have to be some type of nuclear bomb dropped in order to bring such desolation worse than Pearl Harbor.

Each New Year's Eve in New York City we celebrate a new year approaching and the old year departing with a huge ball falling in Time Square at midnight. How symbolic is that? This 7th vial judgment will occur on the eve of the Son of Man returning and the approaching of the 8th year or day (one thousand years) which is the Millennium. Just like men celebrating New Year's Eve by drinking and partying, so shall it be when the Son of Man comes (Matthew 24:36-39). In the parable of the ten virgins, the bridegroom comes at midnight at a time least expected (Matthew 25:1-13). No man knows the day nor the hour. And so shall it be when the Son of Man returns (Matt 24:34-39; Mark 13:31-33). Wake up America and repent of all our pride, idolatry, and unrighteousness.

There fell upon men great hail out of heaven with every stone weighing about the weight of a talent which is seventy to one hundred pounds. This event is referring to Jerusalem and not Mystery Babylon and occurs before the Second Advent of Jesus, The Chief Cornerstone. The men blasphemed God because the plague of the hail was exceeding great (Revelation 11:19). This event is prophesied in Isaiah the 28th chapter.

Isaiah 28:14-18 (KJV)

[14] *"Wherefore hear the word of the Lord, ye scornful men, that rule this people which is in Jerusalem.*

Chapter Sixteen

¹⁵ Because ye have said, We have made a covenant with death, and with hell are we at agreement; when the overflowing scourge shall pass through, it shall not come unto us: for we have made lies our refuge, and under falsehood have we hid ourselves:

¹⁶ Therefore thus saith the Lord God, Behold, I lay in Zion for a foundation a stone, a tried stone, a precious corner stone, a sure foundation: he that believeth shall not make haste.

¹⁷ Judgment also will I lay to the line, and righteousness to the plummet: and the hail shall sweep away the refuge of lies, and the waters shall overflow the hiding place.

¹⁸ And your covenant with death shall be disannulled, and your agreement with hell shall not stand; when the overflowing scourge shall pass through, then ye shall be trodden down by it."

CHAPTER SEVENTEEN

There came one of the seven angels which had the seven vials and talked with John saying, *"Come hither; I will shew unto thee the judgment of the great whore that sitteth upon many waters: With whom the kings of the earth have committed fornication, and the inhabitants of the earth have been made drunk with the wine of her fornication."* Then he carried John away in the spirit into the wilderness. He sees a woman sitting upon a scarlet colored beast, full of names of blasphemy, having seven heads and ten horns. The woman is arrayed in purple and scarlet color. She is decked with gold and precious stones and pearls. She has a golden cup in her hand full of abominations and the filthiness of her fornication. Upon her forehead was a name written, MYSTERY, BABYLON THE GREAT, THE MOTHER OF HARLOTS AND ABOMINATIONS OF THE EARTH.

The Statue of Liberty (Libertas)

Does this woman remind you of anyone? The Statue of Liberty (*Liberty Enlightening the World*) bears these characteristics. The statue is a robed female figure

Chapter Seventeen

representing the Roman goddess, Libertas (Liberty). She is a gift from France. According to American history, there were a lot of financial troubles funding her pedestal. Obviously, God did not want her placed there. She is made of copper (the color of red blood smeared) similar to the color of the blood moons. She has a golden (glowing) torch (a torch that looks like a cup) in her hand full of abominations and filthiness of her fornication. Her theme is "Come to her and she will give you rest (idolatry)." Jesus says in Matthew 11:28-30, *"Come unto Me, all ye that labour and are heavy laden, and I will give you rest. Take My yoke upon you, and learn of Me; for I Am meek and lowly in heart: and ye shall find rest unto your souls. For My yoke is easy, and My burden is light."* According to The World Book Encyclopedia (1989), the Statue of Liberty wears a crown with seven spikes that stands for the light of liberty shining on the seven seas and seven continents, the entire world. She has a tablet in her left hand bearing the date of the Declaration of Independence along with a broken chain at the base of her feet representing freedom.

John sees the woman drunken with the blood of the saints and with the blood of the martyrs (or witnesses) of Jesus. When John sees her, he wondered with great admiration. The angel said to him, *"Wherefore didst thou marvel? I will tell thee the mystery of the woman, and of the beast that carrieth her, which hath the seven heads and ten horns. The beast that thou sawest was, and is not; and shall ascend out of the bottomless pit, and go into perdition: and they that dwell on the earth shall wonder, whose names were not written in the book of life from the foundation of the world, when they behold the beast that was, and is not, and yet is. And here is the mind which hath wisdom. The seven heads are seven mountains, on which the woman sitteth. And there are seven kings: five are fallen, and one is, and the other is not yet come; and when he cometh, he must continue a short space. And the beast that was, and is not, even he is the eighth, and is of the seven, and goeth into perdition. And the ten horns which thou sawest are ten kings, which have received no kingdom as yet; but receive power as kings one hour with the beast. These have one mind, and shall give their power and strength unto the beast. These shall make war with the Lamb, and the Lamb shall overcome them: for He is Lord of lords, and King of kings: and they that are with Him are called, and chosen, and faithful."*

Nebuchadnezzar's Image & Daniel's 70 Weeks

To understand the mystery of the woman and the seven kings: five are fallen, and one is, and the other is not yet come, we must understand the image that Nebuchadnezzar saw in the book of Daniel. These Gentile kingdom empires once ruled and will rule over the nation of Judah and the city of Jerusalem. The below chart is a representation of these kingdom empires prophesied in the book of Daniel.

Chapter Seventeen

Nebuchadnezzar's Image Chart Book of Daniel - Chapters 2, 7, & 9	
Image Empires	**Daniel 70 Weeks**
Gold - Babylonians (Head) (Judah 70 years Captivity)	7 Weeks = **49 years** From 586 BC - Fall of Jerusalem To 537 BC - Cyrus Decree to Rebuild **(No Temple sacrifices made in Jerusalem. Temple was destroyed. They were taken to Babylon.)**
Silver - Medes & Persians (Breast & Arms) **539 – 336 BC** Brass (Bronze) – Greeks Alexander III (Belly) The Seleucids (Antiochus Epiphanes) (Thigh) The Ptolomies (Thigh) **336 - 163 BC**	62 Weeks = **434 total years** From 539 BC - Medes & Persians, Greeks, and Romans To 5 BC - Birth of Jesus (The Messiah) Caesar Augustus Decree to Taxed *Minus* the Maccabean Revolt & Hasmonean Dynasty Years **163 -63 BC (100 years)** or **161 -63 BC (98 years)** 161 BC Roman Jewish Treaty signed
Iron - Rome (Legs) (East & West) **63 BC to 5 BC (The Birth of Jesus, the Messiah)**	This time period is *not* included: Birth of Messiah to Messiah's Death & Resurrection to the Rapture of Church **5 BC to The Week of Daniel**

Chapter Seventeen

Iron Mixed ^{w}/Clay (Feet) United Nations (USA) (Includes the Vatican & the Ten Kings aka Mystery Babylon)	The Week of Daniel 1 week = **7 years** The Great Tribulation is the last 3 ½ years **To Come**
All events have occurred except the last week. All dates are approximate.	

Chapter Seventeen

The above chart is a reflection of the image shown to Nebuchadnezzar in a dream in response to his thoughts as to what was going to become of his kingdom in the latter days (Daniel 2:28-29). The Lord showed him that his kingdom will be overthrown by the Medes/Persians, then the Greeks, then the Romans, then the Antichrist and ten kings, and finally The Greatest King of all, The Word of God (Jesus). The image consists of all of the *Gentile* kingdoms who enslaved or ruled over (the body) and who will enslave or rule over (the feet) Jerusalem and Israel until the Second Coming of Jesus are indicated on this image. The stone that is cut out without hands will in the future smite those kingdoms and break them into pieces. Jesus Christ, the Word of God, (The Chief Cornerstone is also known as The Stone That The Builders Rejected) is that stone (Daniel 2:44-45). The final kingdom to rule is that of our Lord Jesus in His Millennial kingdom. Jerusalem is the Lord's Holy City in which He put His Name upon.

Nebuchadnezzar's image is called the Times of the Gentiles including the last week (3 ½ years) which is called the Time of Jacob's Trouble or Great Tribulation. The image does not include the time period for the Maccabean Dynasty, the Hasmonean Dynasty, the Messiah's First Advent (Jesus, King, and Lord at birth – Matthew 2:2; Luke 2:11), Jesus' earthly ministry, and the current church age. This image in Daniel chapter 2 is made of gold, silver, brass or bronze, iron, and iron/clay. It is reflective of Judah's continual disobedience which led to their captivity for 70 years and 70 weeks (490 years). Seventy is the number associated with forgiveness and seventy times seven is

Chapter Seventeen

the number for complete forgiveness (Matthew 18:21-22). When the four hundred and ninety years are finished, Israel will be completely forgiven and restored. Part of the seventy years of Babylonian captivity is included in the seventy weeks which are 47 years.

Because of Judah's idolatry and continual disobedience to the Lord's command, they provoked the Lord to anger (Jeremiah 25:1-14). He told them to serve Nebuchadnezzar, King of Babylon, and not to rebel against Nebuchadnezzar (Jeremiah 27). When King Zedekiah caused Judah to rebel in captivity to Nebuchadnezzar, Jerusalem was destroyed and burned which is the Fall of Jerusalem in 586 BC (Jeremiah 52:3-27). They were in Babylonian captivity for 70 years before the Medes and Persians conquered Babylon (Jeremiah 25:11-12; Daniel 5).

In Daniel 9:24-27 says, *"Seventy weeks are determined upon thy people and upon thy holy city, to finish the transgression, and to make an end of sins, and to make reconciliation for iniquity, and to bring in everlasting righteousness, and to seal up the vision and prophecy, and to anoint the most Holy. Know therefore and understand, that from the going forth of the commandment to restore and to build Jerusalem unto the Messiah the Prince shall be seven weeks, and threescore and two weeks: the street shall be built again, and the wall, even in troublous times. And after threescore and two weeks shall Messiah be cut off, but not for Himself: and the people of the prince that shall come shall destroy the city and the sanctuary; and the end thereof shall be with a flood, and unto the end of the war desolations are*

Chapter Seventeen

determined." And he shall confirm the covenant with many for one week: and in the midst of the week he shall cause the sacrifice and the oblation to cease, and for the overspreading of abominations he shall make it desolate, even until the consummation, and that determined shall be poured upon the desolate."

These verses lets us know that seventy groupings of seven (weeks) or 490 years have been determined for Jerusalem and all of the Israelites (Israel and Judah) to finish the transgression, to make an end of sins, to make reconciliation for iniquity, and to bring in everlasting righteousness, to seal up the vision and prophecy, and to anoint the most Holy.

Forty-nine years (7 weeks of sevens) will elapse prior to the issuance of the decree by Cyrus to restore and to build Jerusalem. Judah did not have a temple to worship in and make sacrifices to the Lord God for 49 years because of Zedekiah's rebellion. In 586 BC, Nebuzaradan, captain of the guard, who served the king of Babylon, entered into Jerusalem and burned the house of the Lord, the king's house, the houses of the great men, and all the houses of Jerusalem. All of the walls around Jerusalem were broken down. He took some of the people back to Babylon in exile and left a few poor people to work the vineyards and fields (Jeremiah 52:3-27; 2nd Chronicles 36).

From the proclamation of the decree to rebuild given by Cyrus to the birth of Jesus (Messiah the Prince) shall be sixty-two weeks of sevens (434 years) in which the temple, the streets, and the wall will be built again in

Chapter Seventeen

troublous times. In 537 BC, Cyrus, King of Persia, issued a decree for the people of Israel to return to Jerusalem to rebuild the temple and Jerusalem (Ezra 1:1-4).

After 434 years (sixty-two weeks of sevens), the Messiah (Jesus) will be cut off (crucified), but not for Himself. First John 3:5 says, *"And ye know that He was manifested to take away our sins; and in Him is no sin."* Second Corinthians 5:21 says, *"For He made Him Who knew no sin to be sin for us, that we might become the righteousness of God in Him."* And Jesus said in Luke 24:46-47, *"And said unto them, Thus it is written, and thus it behooved Christ to suffer, and to rise from the dead the third day: And that repentance and remission of sins should be preached in His name among all nations, beginning at Jerusalem."*

The people of the prince will come and destroy the city and the sanctuary which Jesus spoke about in the gospels (Matthew 24:2; Mark 13:27; Luke 21:6). The end will be with a flood, not of water, but of blood at the end of the war (Gog and Magog) at the Messiah's Second Coming. The Antichrist will confirm a covenant with many for one week (7 years) and in the middle of the week (3 ½ years), he will break the covenant. He will cause the sacrifice and the oblation to cease. Because of the overspreading of abominations, he shall make it desolate until the consummation, and all of that determined shall be poured upon the desolate.

Chapter Seventeen

The purpose of the following table is to identify the 49 years, the 434 years, and last 7 years.*

Dates	Explanation	Scripture Reference
605 BC	Nebuchadnezzar II enters Jerusalem as king.	Jeremiah 25:1-13; Daniel 1:1-2; Daniel 7
598 BC	Jehoiachin (Jeconiah), rebelled and reigned 3 mos. 10 days (1 year.)	2nd Chronicles 36:9-10
597-586 BC	Zedekiah ruled under Nebuchadnezzar II for 11 years.	Jeremiah 52:1-16; 2nd Chronicles 36:10-11
586 BC	Fall of Jerusalem – Zedekiah rebels against Nebuchadnezzar II (in the 19th year) and Jerusalem is burned (desolate.)	Jeremiah 27;52:3-27; 2nd Chronicles 36:10-21
586-537 BC	<u>49 years</u> elapsed (temple destroyed - no sacrifices made) until Cyrus' (King of Persia) decree for the people to return and rebuild the temple in Jerusalem.	Ezra 1:1-4
539-537	<u>2 years</u> Belshazzar king of the Chaldeans was slain by Darius the Mede. - KJV bible pg. 1281;	Daniel 5:30-31; Ezra 1:1 Comments

Chapter Seventeen

	Ezra 1:1 comments in KJV Bible states that Cyrus conquered Babylon with Ugbaru on October 12, 539 KJV bible pg. 756.	
537-336 BC	<u>201 years</u> Medes & Persian Empires	Daniel chapters 2, 7, 8, 9
336-163 BC	<u>173 years</u> Grecian Empire Comments : Dates are from: a.) Daniel 11:3,4 in KJV bible pg. 1291; b.) Daniel 8:9 in KJV bible pg. 1285.	Daniel chapters 2, 7, 8, 9
163-63 BC or 161-63 BC	This time period is not included on the image in Daniel 2. It is the Maccabean Revolt & Hasmonean Dynasty. 161 BC Roman Jewish Treaty signed	
63 BC to the Birth of Messiah (Jesus) 5 BC	<u>58 years</u> The seventy weeks end with the birth of Jesus. Comments : Dates are from: Matthew 2:12-18 in KJV bible pg. 1407 Herod the Great died in 4 BC.	Matthew 2; Luke 2:1-14

Chapter Seventeen

To Come	The last <u>7 years</u> in which 3 ½ years are the Great Tribulation period known as the Time Of Jacob's Trouble and occur prior to the Second Advent of Jesus (The Word Of God.)	Daniel 2, 8, 9, 12:1; Revelation 12, 13, 17; Jeremiah 30:7; Matthew 24:21-22; Mark 13:19-20;
*All events have occurred except the last week. All dates are approximate.		

Chapter Seventeen

"The beast that thou sawest was, and is not; and shall ascend out of the bottomless pit, and go into perdition: and they that dwell on the earth shall wonder, whose names were not written in the book of life from the foundation of the world, when they behold the beast that was, and is not, and yet is. And here is the mind which hath wisdom. The seven heads are seven mountains, on which the woman sitteth."

The beast that thou sawest was, and is not; and shall ascend out of the bottomless pit, and go into perdition is the Antichrist, a future fallen pope. They that dwell on the earth shall wonder, whose names were not written in the book of life from the foundation of the world when they behold the Antichrist. Here is the mind which hath wisdom. The seven heads are seven mountains, on which the woman sitteth. This event occurs during the great tribulation after the rapture of the church. He will have influence with those dwelling upon the earth. The seven heads/mountains are the entire seven continents (entire world) on which the woman (Mystery Babylon) sits.

"And there are seven kings: five are fallen, and one is, and the other is not yet come; and when he cometh, he must continue a short space. And the beast that was, and is not, even he is the eighth, and is of the seven, and goeth into perdition. And the ten horns which thou sawest are ten kings, which have received no kingdom as yet; but receive power as kings one hour with the beast. These have one mind, and shall give their power and strength unto the beast. These shall make war with the Lamb, and the Lamb shall overcome them: for He is Lord of lords,

Chapter Seventeen

and King of kings: and they that are with Him are called, and chosen, and faithful."

There are *seven kings* of which five are fallen, and one is, and the other is not yet come; and when he cometh, he must continue a short space. The five fallen kings (kingdoms) are the Assyrians, Egyptians, Babylonians, Medes and Persians, and the Greeks. On the image in the book of Daniel chapter two, the head of fine gold was *Babylon*, his breast and arms of silver were the *Medes* and *Persians*, his belly of brass or bronze (Alexander III the Great - *Greece*) and his thighs of brass or bronze (Ptolemy - *Greece* and Antiochus IV Epiphanes - *Greece*), his legs of iron (*Rome*), his feet are part iron (Rome and the Vatican City) and part clay (ten kings and nations). The Vatican City is a small independent state inside the city of Rome, Italy. The ten kings that have not received a kingdom as of yet represents the part of clay and are from the old Grecian Empire that conquered the Medes and Persian Empire.

The king that is considered "one is", in this chapter, is Rome the seventh. At the time of John's writing, Rome was ruling over the Jews in Jerusalem. The beast that was, and is not, even he is the eighth, and is of the seven, and goes into perdition is the fallen pope out of the State of the Vatican. The State of the Vatican City is a state located within the city of Rome. The ten horns are ten kings, which have not received a kingdom as of yet; but receive power as kings one hour with the beast (Antichrist). They are in complete agreement and unified as having "one mind" and will give their power and strength to the Antichrist. They will make war with the Lamb (the Word of God) at His Second Advent. The Lamb will overcome them because He is God and has come to deliver the entire nation of Israel and the city of Jerusalem. He is the Lord of lords and the King of kings. They that are with Him are called, chosen, and faithful (His saints) (Zechariah 14:5; Jude 1:14-15). All of His holy angels will also return with Him (Matthew 24:31).

To understand Mystery Babylon, we need to reference the Tower of Babel.

The Tower of Babel

Genesis 11:1-9 - The Tower of Babel

¹ And the whole earth was of one language, and of one speech.

² And it came to pass, as they journeyed from the east, that they found a plain in the land of Shinar; and they dwelt there.

³ And they said one to another, Go to, let us make brick, and burn them thoroughly. And they had brick for stone, and slime had they for morter.

⁴ And they said, Go to, let us build us a city and a tower, whose top may reach unto heaven; and let us make us a name, lest we be scattered abroad upon the face of the whole earth.

⁵ And the Lord came down to see the city and the tower, which the children of men builded.

Chapter Seventeen

⁶ And the Lord said, Behold, the people is one, and they have all one language; and this they begin to do: and now nothing will be restrained from them, which they have imagined to do.

⁷ Go to, let us go down, and there confound their language, that they may not understand one another's speech.

⁸ So the Lord scattered them abroad from thence upon the face of all the earth: and they left off to build the city.

⁹ Therefore is the <u>name of it called Babel</u>; because the Lord did there confound the language of all the earth: and from thence did the Lord scatter them abroad upon the face of all the earth.

Babylon in Hebrew is the word babel which means "confusion." In Genesis, the 11ᵗʰ chapter, Babel (Babylon) is a plain in the land of Shinar. It was there that the Lord did confound the language of all the earth and scattered them abroad upon the face of all the earth. They had said one to another, *"Let us build us a city and a tower, whose top may reach unto heaven and let us make us a name, lest we be scattered abroad upon the face of the whole earth."* The Lord had clearly told Noah and his sons (descendants) to *"Be fruitful, and multiply, and replenish the earth."* He did not tell them to stay in one place, build a tower, and make a name for themselves. He told Abraham that He will make his name great (Genesis 12:2). Disobedience is rebellion. First Samuel 15:23 says, *"For rebellion is as the sin of witchcraft, and stubbornness is as iniquity and idolatry. Because thou hast rejected the word of the Lord, He hath*

Chapter Seventeen

also rejected thee from being king." The Lord came down to see the city and the tower which the children of men had built. Then, the Lord said, *"Behold, the people is one, and they have all one language; and this they begin to do: and now nothing will be restrained from them, which they have imagined to do. Go to, let us go down, and there confound their language, that they may not understand one another's speech."*

Mystery Babylon

Then he says to John, *"The waters which thou sawest, where the whore sitteth, are peoples, and multitudes, and nations, and tongues. And the ten horns which thou sawest upon the beast, these shall hate the whore, and shall make her desolate and naked, and shall eat her flesh, and burn her with fire. For God hath put in their hearts to fulfil His will, and to agree, and give their kingdom unto the beast, until the words of God shall be fulfilled. And the woman which thou sawest is that great city, which reigneth over the kings of the earth."*

MYSTERY BABYLON THE GREAT, THE MOTHER OF HARLOTS AND ABOMINATIONS OF THE EARTH is New York City, New York located in the United States of America. Mystery Babylon is a city and not a country. New York City is where the Statue of Liberty and The Headquarters of the United Nations are located. New York's coat of arms and state flag clearly depicts the Mystery Babylon mentioned in the 5th chapter of the book of Zechariah. According to World Book Encyclopedia, New York City was the temporary capital of the United States in January 1785.

Chapter Seventeen

The United States was once under English rule. Her governing body nickname is known as Uncle Sam. To see pictures of New York's State flag and seal, please reference New York State in an encyclopedia or search online. These symbols were prophesied in the bible.

In Zechariah 5:6-11 states, *"This is an ephah that goeth forth. He said moreover, This is their resemblance through all the earth. And, behold, there was lifted up a talent of lead: and this is a woman that sitteth in the midst of the ephah. And he said, This is wickedness. And he cast it into the midst of the ephah; and he cast the weight of lead upon the mouth thereof. Then lifted I up mine eyes, and looked, and, behold, there came out two women, and the wind was in their wings; for they had wings like the wings of a stork: and they lifted up the ephah between the earth and the heaven. Then said I to the angel that talked with me, Whither do these bear the ephah? And he said unto me, To build it an house in the land of Shinar (Babylon): and it shall be established, and set there upon her own base."*

The woman in the ephah represents Wickedness or Evil. He cast her back down into the middle of the ephah and placed a lead cover on its opening. There are two women (supporters) with wings (capes) and appear on New York State's coat of arms and state flag. According to New York's state history, these two supporters are called Liberty and Justice. They are not angels. Remember that Liberty is a Roman goddess. They lifted up the ephah between the earth and the heaven representing Satan's kingdom and his influence on mankind to be their own type of god. Ephesian 2:2-3 states, *"Wherein in time past ye walked according to the*

Chapter Seventeen

course of this world, according to the prince of the power of the air, the spirit that now worketh in the children of disobedience: Among whom also we all had our conversation in times past in the lusts of our flesh, fulfilling the desires of the flesh and of the mind; and were by nature the children of wrath, even as others." The prophet Zechariah asked the angel "Where are they taking the ephah?" The angel response to the prophet was to build Wickedness a house in the land of Shinar (Mystery Babylon) and that Wickedness shall be established and set there upon her (Statue of Liberty- the Roman goddess, Libertas) own base (pedestal). According to The World Book Encyclopedia (1989), the Statue of Liberty wears a crown with seven spikes that stands for the light of liberty shining on the seven seas and seven continents (entire earth). The golden eagle is The Headquarters of the United Nation's Security Council located in New York City, USA. On New York State flag, the golden eagle is sitting on the entire earth in which the United Nations Security Council will rule in Mystery Babylon over all nations. All nations will look to them for relief and prosperity, therefore causing idolatry and wickedness (<u>**Daniel chapter 7 first beast – Mystery Babylon also known as New York City; the fourth beast – The Headquarters of the United Nation's Security Council**</u>). God wants only God, the Heavenly Father, to be worshipped via His Son, Jesus, and to bring relief (liberty), peace, and prosperity (the 1st Commandment). The 1st Commandment is to love God with all of our heart, mind, body, and soul. This statement is *especially true* for the nation of Israel, His bride. The church will be raptured during the great tribulation.

Daniel 7 - The Fourth Beast - The Headquarters of the United Nations

The Headquarters of the United Nations, made up of nearly two hundred nations, resides over the kingdoms/nations of the earth keeping world peace and security among all the nations. Therefore, a "one-world" type of government created to keep the peace over all of the nations/kingdoms on the seven continents (heads). The United States of America does not own The Headquarters of the United Nations nor do they own the land that it sits upon. They are not governed by The United States of America. Their headquarters is located in the Manhattan borough in New York City. The seven heads are the seven mountains (continents – entire world) on which the woman sits. According to the scripture, the waters represent peoples, multitudes, nations, and tongues (also known as the nations/entire world).

The beast that the woman sits upon represents the fourth beast mentioned in Daniel 7:7-8, 19-26 which says, *"After this I saw in the night visions, and behold a fourth beast, dreadful and terrible, and strong exceedingly; and it had great iron teeth: it devoured and brake in pieces, and stamped the residue with the feet of it: and it was diverse from all the beasts that were before it; and it had ten horns. I considered the horns, and, behold, there came up among them another little horn, before whom there were three of the first horns plucked*

Chapter Seventeen

up by the roots: and, behold, in this horn were eyes like the eyes of man, and a mouth speaking great things...Then I would know the truth of the fourth beast, which was diverse from all the others, exceeding dreadful, whose teeth were of iron, and his nails of brass; which devoured, brake in pieces, and stamped the residue with his feet; And of the ten horns that were in his head, and of the other which came up, and before whom three fell; even of that horn that had eyes, and a mouth that spake very great things, whose look was more stout than his fellows. I beheld, and the same horn made war with the saints, and prevailed against them; Until the Ancient of days came, and judgment was given to the saints of the most High; and the time came that the saints possessed the kingdom. Thus he said, The fourth beast shall be the fourth kingdom upon earth, which shall be diverse from all kingdoms, and shall devour the whole earth, and shall tread it down, and break it in pieces. And the ten horns out of this kingdom are ten kings that shall arise: and another shall rise after them; and he shall be diverse from the first, and he shall subdue three kings. And he shall speak great words against the most High, and shall wear out the saints of the most High, and think to change times and laws: and they shall be given into his hand until a time and times and the dividing of time. But the judgment shall sit, and they shall take away his dominion, to consume and to destroy it unto the end."

This fourth beast is The Headquarters of United Nations Security Council located in New York City, New York in the United States of America in which the Antichrist (the little horn) will be a part of (Daniel 7:7). This beast is a dreadful, terrible, and exceedingly strong only because of the measures needed to be taken to keep peace and security via the United Nations Security Council. It devoured and broke in pieces, and stamped the residue with the feet of it. It is diverse from all the other beasts that were before it. This beast is different from the other beasts because it is a one-world governmental body consisting of hundreds of nations trying to keep world peace. The beast has iron teeth (many nations) with each nation able to devour and crush. Daniel saw The UN Security Council Chamber in New York City made up of 15 member nations that vote on actions to be taken in cases of strife between nations to grant peace. There is a section at the front of the room that resembles a model of the human teeth. It is shaped like a horseshoe with many chairs. Iron in scripture represents Rome which is a member of The Headquarters of the United Nations.

The pedestal is surrounded by a base just like the city of Rome surrounds the State of the Vatican City. The Vatican City is a small independent city/state. The pedestal that the Statue of Liberty sits upon resembles an upper molar (tooth). This tooth is a representation of a future fallen pope who goes into perdition during the great tribulation (Revelation 17:3, 8). The future fallen pope is the little horn that rises up from The Headquarters of the United Nations (Daniel 7:8, 19-20). He resides in the State of the Vatican City (with statehood) located in the city of Rome, Italy. The pedestal at one time used to have cast iron steps until 1933. Iron represents the Roman Empire on Nebuchadnezzar image.

Chapter Seventeen

The beast has ten horns which are ten kings. They are members of The Headquarters of the United Nations as well (Daniel 7:7-8, 19-20). The windows on the base look like brass (bronze) and represent the toenails which are the ten kings that were a part of the Grecian Empire that conquered the Medes and Persian Empire. From within The Headquarters of the United Nations, the Antichrist (little horn or man of sin) arises by whom three of the first horns (kings) were plucked up by the roots. To be plucked up by the roots in Strong's Concordance is "aqar" and means "to be rooted up" (Daniel 7:8). In Daniel 11:42-43, *"He shall stretch forth his hand also upon the countries: and the land of Egypt shall not escape. But he shall have power over the treasures of gold and of silver, and over all the precious things of Egypt: and the Libyans and the Ethiopians shall be at his steps."* Therefore, this refers to Egypt, Libya, and Ethiopia. The area that is called Ethiopia is actually Sudan on the old Medes and Persian map.

"Behold, in this horn were eyes like the eyes of man." The eyes like the eyes of a man mean "to see" and refer to his seat (Daniel 7:8, 20). According to Webster's Third New International Dictionary, the word "see" comes from the Latin word "sedes" meaning the seat or center of power or authority of a bishop a diocesan center. The Antichrist's seat of authority is referred to as the "The Holy See". The fifth angel pours out his vial upon the seat of the beast (a future fallen pope/the Antichrist) because this future fallen pope goes into perdition. His kingdom is full of darkness (Revelation 16:10). He has a mouth speaking great things meaning

blasphemy (Daniel chapters 7; 11; and 12). He will sign a seven-year covenant and break the covenant after the first forty-two months (Daniel 9:27). He opposes and exalts himself above all gods including God the Father. The Antichrist will stand in the temple of God and declare himself as god. This act is known as the abomination of desolation spoken by Daniel the prophet. Jesus says for those in Judea to flee to the mountains without hesitation when they see the abomination of desolation (Matthew 24:15-22; Mark 13:14-20; Luke 21:20-22). The Antichrist will cause the daily sacrifices and the oblation to cease.

There are some in the Catholic Church that refers to him as the Holy Father. We know that there is only one Holy Father and He is God the Father. I must mention that I have never heard a pope refer to himself as god or Holy Father. However, this future fallen pope will believe that he is god. Popes are considered to be men of peace. As believers in Jesus Christ, we know that Jesus, the Christ, is the Head of the Church consisting of believing Jews and Gentiles which He purchased with His precious Blood at Calvary.

During the Antichrist time of reigning, he will be a conqueror until his time of reigning is up. The Antichrist will make war with the saints, including the two witnesses, who are prophets, and other nations and he will overcome them (Revelation 11). He will make war until the Ancient of Days, Who is Jesus, comes. Jesus, the Word of God, comes at His Second Advent and defeats the Antichrist and his false prophet and throws them alive into the lake of fire. Then, judgment

Chapter Seventeen

will be given to the saints of the Most High and the saints will possess the kingdom (Millennium). Zechariah 12:10-11 says, *"And I will pour upon the house of David, and upon the inhabitants of Jerusalem, the spirit of grace and of supplications: and they shall look upon Me Whom they have pierced, and they shall mourn for Him, as one mourneth for his only son, and shall be in bitterness for Him, as one that is in bitterness for his firstborn. In that day shall there be a great mourning in Jerusalem, as the mourning of Hadadrimmon in the valley of Megiddon."*

Back to the text...

The ten kings that were once members of The Headquarters of the United Nations hate the whore (Mystery Babylon also known as New York City). She is called a whore because of her infidelity to God via her pride, wickedness, idolatry, and false worship. In one hour, they shall make her desolate and naked. They shall eat her flesh and burn her with fire because God put into their hearts to fulfill His will, to agree, and give their kingdom to the beast (Antichrist) until the words of God's prophecy be fulfilled. The woman that John saw is that great city (Mystery Babylon) that reigns over the kings of the earth. After the fall of Mystery Babylon, these ten kings have one mind and shall give their power and strength to the Antichrist.

The United States of America is a nation that was born or birthed on godly principles. It was founded by Christians who were seeking freedom. As a nation, we have allowed confusion to enter our country. We need to repent and return to the God of our fathers.

Chapter Seventeen

Confusion is a word that clearly defines our world today as we slowly apostatize (fall away). We say in God we trust and that we are a Christian nation yet we pass laws/legislation contrary to the Word of God. Nowhere, is it written in the Constitution of the United States of America the words Christ, Messiah, Savior, or Jesus (words which denote Christianity.) We are not a Christian nation. To make my point clear, would we call your home a Christian home if within each bedroom a different religion was practiced? No, we would not. We are a nation that has some Christians living within just like other nations. The scripture states in 1st Corinthians 6:9-11, *"Know ye not that the unrighteous shall not inherit the kingdom of God? Be not deceived: neither fornicators, nor idolaters, nor adulterers, nor effeminate, nor abusers of themselves with mankind, Nor thieves, nor covetous, nor drunkards, nor revilers, nor extortioners, shall inherit the kingdom of God. And such were some of you: but ye are washed, but ye are sanctified, but ye are justified in the name of the Lord Jesus, and by the Spirit of our God."*

We have played the harlot when our nation's Supreme Court approved same-sex marriages and legalized abortions. God clearly defines marriage between a male and female. He said, *"Let every man has his own wife."* I am not being prejudiced against the homosexual or the person who had an abortion, but I must tell the truth because a soul is at stake. As a Christian, we are charged to love all mankind (meaning everyone also referred to as your neighbor) and hate sin. We are to be followers of Jesus, the Christ, and His teachings. However, I am against legalizing what God calls sin in His Holy Bible.

According to Leviticus chapters 18 & 20, homosexuality is an abomination that defiles the individual and the nation (land) causing God to visit the iniquity upon the people and the land. In America, there are all gay <u>practicing</u> congregations. In Romans 1:26-28 says, *"For this cause God gave them up unto vile affections: for even their women did change the natural use into that which is against nature: And likewise also the men, leaving the natural use of the woman, burned in their lust one toward another; men with men working that which is unseemly, and receiving in themselves that recompence of their error which was meet. And even as they did not like to retain God in their knowledge, God gave them over to a reprobate mind, to do those things which are not convenient."* Jesus died for all sins including homosexuality. A person can be forgiven of homosexuality if they repent and turn (sin no more) from this act just like fornication and any other sin. Remember that a person that <u>practices</u> sin is a sinner. The only sin that a person cannot be forgiven for is the sin of blasphemy and that is rejecting the only way of escape from sin which is through the blood of Jesus, the crucified Lamb of God. Though our sins may be as scarlet, they shall be as white as snow. Though they are red like crimson, they shall be as wool. He will forgive the sinner and remember their sin no more. All sin debt was paid in full by Jesus. He paid the full penalty for our sins. All we have to do is believe on Him and His finished works at Calvary and receive Him as our Savior and Lord.

Chapter Seventeen

As Christians, we are to be a watchman. After receiving the truth ourselves, we are mandated to tell the world and the church the truth so that they (the individual) will repent of their sins and be saved. If not, their blood will be on our hands (Ezekiel chapters 3, 18, and 33). There is hope for all sinners who repent knowing that all of us were born sinners. The bible says that where sin abounded the grace of God is greater (Romans 5:30). In Christ, the repentant sinner can be forgiven of all of their sins and cleansed from all unrighteousness (sin). God will not remember their sins anymore and they are justified as if they never sinned. To whom the Son sets free from sin is free indeed (John 8:31-36). The scripture also says in Romans 8:33, *"Who shall lay any thing to the charge of God's elect? It is God that justifieth."*

There are people changing their gender because Satan has convinced them that something is wrong with their God-given gender and that they should be the opposite gender. As if to say, God in all of His omnipotence and omniscience would and could make a mistake when He chose each person's gender. He did not make a mistake when He chose each person's gender. He is a purposeful God. He specifically chose our gender with His purpose in mind. Satan is a liar and a deceiver according to the scripture. Every person is created in the image and likeness of God Almighty. Satan is jealous because he wanted to be like the Most High God and was cut down to the ground (Isaiah 14:14). When God created man, He created them male and female and He knew exactly what He was doing.

Chapter Seventeen

Satan wants individuals to rebel against God and leave their God giving gender and choose the opposite gender and be in rebellion (sin) against God. Fallen angels did the same thing during the time of Noah when they (the sons of God) took for themselves wives of all which they chose (Genesis 6:2). The book of Jude also tells us that the angels, who kept not their first estate but left their own habitation He hath reserved in everlasting chains under darkness until the judgment of the great day (Jude 1:6). How do you know that they were fallen angels? In the book of Job chapters 1 & 2, the term sons of God refer to angels. The bible also refers to saints as sons of God because we were created by Him. John 1:12 says, *"But as many as received Him, to them gave He power to become the sons of God, even to them that believe on His name."*

People are also positioning themselves in the place of God by freezing of fertilizing embryos via the in-vitro fertilization process. Are we God? Has God given us the ability to decide who gets to be born and who does not? God told man before and after the flood to *"Be fruitful, and multiply, and replenish the earth."* **To disregard this command is to openly rebel along with committing murder. He was not just referring only to the care of the earth, but to man's reproduction, as well as, everything living thing in the earth. Babies, in embryo or fetus form, are being aborted instead of being given an opportunity to live and be placed for adoption. Wake up! There is nothing wrong with adoption. As Christians, we were adopted into the family of God by Way of His Son, Jesus. Ephesians 1:3-6 says it best,** *"Blessed be the God and Father of our*

Chapter Seventeen

Lord Jesus Christ, Who hath blessed us with all spiritual blessings in heavenly places in Christ: According as He <u>hath chosen us in Him before the foundation of the world</u>, that we should be holy and without blame before Him in love: Having <u>predestinated us unto the adoption of children by Jesus Christ to Himself</u>, according to the good pleasure of His will, To the praise of the glory of His grace, wherein He hath made us accepted in the Beloved."

We have removed the Ten Commandments and prayer from a lot of our public venues, as well as, in our public schools along with the name of Jesus (Apostasy). Is this not confusion? Would a Christian nation reject God's Word and His Son? Would Almighty God approve and be pleased with these things? Absolutely not!

After Jesus' death and resurrection, we are not under the curse of the Law of Moses (the Ten Commandments), but we are under grace. The Law of Moses is not a curse. It is holy and is still the Word of God. The transgression against the Law of Moses brings a curse to the transgressor. He still disapproves of these things (sin). Jesus came to fulfill the law and to show us a better way. Yes, the heart way. This Way is the Law of Love. In Matthew 22:33-40, *"And when the multitude heard this, they were astonished at His doctrine. But when the Pharisees had heard that He had put the Sadducees to silence, they were gathered together. Then one of them, which were a lawyer, asked Him a question, tempting Him, and saying, Master, which is the great commandment in the law? Jesus said to him, Thou*

Chapter Seventeen

shalt love the Lord thy God with all thy heart, and with all thy soul, and with all thy mind. This is the first and great commandment. And the second is like unto it, Thou shalt love thy neighbor as thyself. On these two commandments hang all the law and the prophets." If we truly love one another as the scripture states, then we would not transgress against one another and truly love each other.

The scripture clearly gives us hope when it says in 2nd Chronicles 7:14, *"If My people, which are called by My name, shall humble themselves, and pray, and seek My face, and turn from their wicked ways; then will I hear from heaven, and will forgive their sin, and will heal their land."*

In Luke 15:10-32, there is a story about a father that has two sons and he gives them both their inheritance. The younger son leaves his father's home and spends his entire inheritance on what we call "the party life" (riotous living or having fun). Once his money was well spent and a famine arose, he is found in want and homeless. While being homeless, he comes to himself or is reminded of his father's love and how well his father's servants are well cared for. He rehearses his speech of repentance to God and to his father. He journeys to his father's home only to find out that his father is daily watching and waiting for his return. His father greets him with great joy and does not allow him to finish his speech of repentance. His father restored him to the place where he was with his father prior to his leaving. His father threw a great feast to welcome his son home. His father forgave him immediately and

Chapter Seventeen

never discussed his past riotous living and sins with him. The older son was angry and would not attend the feast or party. The oldest son tells the father of his obedience to the father and rehearses his younger brother's sins to the father. The father never discusses his youngest son's sins with the older brother but tells the oldest son to rejoice with them because his brother, who was dead (spiritually), is now alive (born again). He was lost and is now found (saved). Luke 15:10 says, *"Likewise, I say unto you, there is joy in the presence of the angels of God over one sinner that repenteth."* Just as the earthly father forgave his youngest son sins and did not bring them up again, our Heavenly Father does the same thing for us. Once a person repents, God the Father remembers their sins no more. Satan is the accuser of the brethren and will remind you of your sins often in order to bring guilt and shame. His purpose is to hinder your spiritual walk with the Lord. Sometimes, he will use others to remind you of your past sins. Allow the Holy Spirit to remind you that you are forgiven and that there is no condemnation to those who are in Christ Jesus who walk after the Spirit and not the flesh (five senses and selfish desires), the old sin nature (Romans 8:1). You can now walk with your head held up, not in pride, but free from the bondage of guilt and shame when the accusers of the brethren come. Second Corinthians 5:17, *"Therefore if any man be in Christ, he is a new creature: old things are passed away; behold, all things are become new."*

CHAPTER EIGHTEEN

Babylon, the Great Is Fallen

After seeing the harlot on the beast, John sees another angel come down from heaven, having great power and the earth was lightened with his glory. He cried mightily with a strong voice saying, *"Babylon the great is fallen, is fallen, and is become the habitation of devils, and the hold of every foul spirit, and a cage of every unclean and hateful bird. For all nations have drunk of the wine of the wrath of her fornication, and the kings of the earth have committed fornication with her, and the merchants of the earth are waxed rich through the abundance of her delicacies."*

Chapter Eighteen

New York City has been destroyed or should I say will be destroyed just like in the day when the Lord destroyed Sodom and Gomorrah. This event will occur just before the Second Advent of Jesus. Her sins ascended up to God just like Sodom and Gomorrah sins.

The scripture states in Genesis 18:20, *"And the Lord said, Because the cry of Sodom and Gomorrah is great, and because their sin is very grievous."* And in Genesis 19:13-15, 24-25, 27-29, *"For we will destroy this place, because the cry of them is waxen great before the face of the Lord; and the Lord hath sent us to destroy it. And Lot went out, and spake unto his sons in law, which married his daughters, and said, Up, get you out of this place; for the Lord will destroy this city. But he seemed as one that mocked unto his sons in law. And when the morning arose, then the angels hastened Lot, saying, Arise, take thy wife, and thy two daughters, which are here; lest thou be consumed in the iniquity of the city…Then the Lord rained upon Sodom and upon Gomorrah brimstone and fire from the Lord out of heaven; And he overthrew those cities, and all the plain, and all the inhabitants of the cities, and that which grew upon the ground…And Abraham gat up early in the morning to the place where he stood before the Lord: And he looked toward Sodom and Gomorrah, and toward all the land of the plain, and beheld, and, lo, the smoke of the country went up as the smoke of a furnace. And it came to pass, when God destroyed the cities of the plain, that God remembered Abraham, and sent Lot out of the midst of*

Chapter Eighteen

the overthrow, when he overthrew the cities in the which Lot dwelt."

Warning to God's Covenanted People

John hears another voice from heaven saying, *"Come out of her, My people, that ye be not partakers of her sins, and that ye receive not of her plagues because her sins have reached unto heaven and God hath remembered her iniquities. Reward her even as she rewarded you, and double unto her double according to her works: in the cup which she hath filled fill to her double. How much she hath glorified herself, and lived deliciously, so much torment and sorrow give her: for she saith in her heart, I sit a queen, and am no widow, and shall see no sorrow. Therefore shall her plagues come in one day, death, and mourning, and famine; and she shall be utterly burned with fire: for strong is the Lord God who judgeth her."*

The angel warns God's covenanted people not to be partakers of Mystery Babylon sins because her sins have reached into the third heaven where God resides. Abraham and Lot were warned of judgment coming to Sodom and Gomorrah (Genesis 18:17-21, 19:13). God is going to reward her double according to all of her evil works. She has glorified herself and lived deliciously (James 5:1-6). Therefore, much torment and sorrow will be given to her. New York City has five boroughs named Manhattan (New York County), The Bronx (Bronx County), Brooklyn (Kings County), Queens (Queens County), and Staten Island (Richmond

Chapter Eighteen

County). She says in her heart, *"I sit a queen, and am no widow, and shall see no sorrow."* She makes this statement because there is no borough named Kings, but there is a Kings County. Her plagues shall come in one day during the seventh vial/bowl judgment resulting in death, mourning, and famine. She will be completely burned with fire. It is the Lord God Who judged her.

The Kings of the Earth Lament for Mystery Babylon

"And the kings of the earth, who have committed fornication and lived deliciously with her, shall bewail her, and lament for her, when they shall see the smoke of her burning, Standing afar off for the fear of her torment, saying, Alas, alas that great city Babylon, that mighty city! for in one hour is thy judgment come."

The kings of the earth (world leaders) who partook of her sins and lived lavishly with her will bewail and lament when they see the smoke from the burning city. They will stand far off for the fear of her torment and say, *"Alas, alas that great city Babylon, that mighty city! for in one hour is the Lord God judgment come."*

The Merchants of the Earth Lament for Mystery Babylon

"And the merchants of the earth shall weep and mourn over her; for no man buyeth their merchandise any more: The merchandise of gold, and silver, and precious stones, and of pearls, and fine linen, and purple, and silk, and scarlet, and all thyine wood, and all manner vessels of

Chapter Eighteen

ivory, and all manner vessels of most precious wood, and of brass, and iron, and marble, And cinnamon, and odours, and ointments, and frankincense, and wine, and oil, and fine flour, and wheat, and beasts, and sheep, and horses, and chariots, and slaves, and souls of men. And the fruits that thy soul lusted after are departed from thee, and all things which were dainty and goodly are departed from thee, and thou shalt find them no more at all. The merchants of these things, which were made rich by her, shall stand afar off for the fear of her torment, weeping and wailing, And saying, Alas, alas that great city, that was clothed in fine linen, and purple, and scarlet, and decked with gold, and precious stones, and pearls!"

The merchants of the earth will weep and mourn over her because no man buys their merchandise any more. These merchants, who were made rich by her, will stand far off because of the fear of her torment. They will be weeping, wailing, and saying, "Alas, alas that great city, that was clothed in fine linen, and purple, and scarlet, and decked with gold, and precious stones, and pearls!"

The Shipmaster of the Earth Lament for Mystery Babylon

"For in one hour so great riches is come to nought. And every shipmaster, and all the company in ships, and sailors, and as many as trade by sea, stood afar off, And cried when they saw the smoke of her burning, saying, What city is like unto this great city! And they cast dust on their heads, and cried, weeping and wailing, saying,

Chapter Eighteen

Alas, alas that great city, wherein were made rich all that had ships in the sea by reason of her costliness! for in one hour is she made desolate."

In one hour, so great riches come to nothing. Every shipmaster, sea traveler (passenger), sailor, and all those that trade by sea will stand far off and say, *"What city is like unto this great city!"* They will cast dust on their heads and will be crying, weeping, wailing, saying, *"Alas, alas that great city, wherein were made rich all that had ships in the sea by reason of her costliness! for in one hour is she made desolate."*

All of Heaven Rejoices Over the Destruction of Mystery Babylon

"Rejoice over her, thou heaven, and ye holy apostles and prophets; for God hath avenged you on her.

All of heaven, the apostles, and the prophets are told to rejoice over the destruction of Mystery Babylon because God Almighty has avenged them.

The Destruction of Mystery Babylon

A mighty angel picked up a stone, like a great millstone, and cast it into the sea saying, *"Thus with violence shall that great city Babylon be thrown down, and shall be found no more at all. And the voice of harpers, and musicians, and of pipers, and trumpeters, shall be heard no more at all in thee; and no craftsman, of whatsoever craft he be, shall be found any more in*

Chapter Eighteen

thee; and the sound of a millstone shall be heard no more at all in thee; And the light of a candle shall shine no more at all in thee; and the voice of the bridegroom and of the bride shall be heard no more at all in thee: for thy merchants were the great men of the earth; for by thy sorceries were all nations deceived. And in her was found the blood of prophets, and of saints, and of all that were slain upon the earth." In one hour, Mystery Babylon will be destroyed by hail (bomb) from the air being dropped in the sea.

(See Revelation Chapter 16 – The 7th Vial Judgment For More Information.)

There will be complete destruction to the point that there will be no more sounds of musical instruments, rejoicing, or craftsman's heard at all. She will be destroyed and rewarded double because of her works: arrogance, deception of all nations by sorceries, the martyrdom of the blood of prophets, the blood of saints, and the blood of all that were slain upon the earth.

CHAPTER NINETEEN

Alleluia Praises in Heaven

After seeing the destruction of Mystery Babylon, John hears a multitude of saints in heaven saying, *"Alleluia! Salvation, and glory, and honour, and power, unto the Lord our God: For true and righteous are His judgments: for He hath judged the great whore, which did corrupt the earth with her fornication, and hath avenged the blood of His servants at her hand."* Again, they shouted, *"Alleluia!"* The smoke from the burning of Mystery Babylon rose up forever and ever. The twenty-four elders and the four beasts fell down and worshipped God that sat on the throne saying, *"Amen! Alleluia!"* A voice proceeded from the throne saying, *"Praise our God, all ye His servants, and ye that fear Him, both small and great!"* Then John hears the voice of a great multitude as the voice of many waters and as the voice of mighty thundering saying, *"Alleluia! For the Lord God Omnipotent reigneth! Let us be glad and rejoice, and give honour to Him: for the Marriage of the Lamb is come, and His wife hath made herself ready! And to her was granted that she should be arrayed in fine linen, clean and white: for the fine linen is the righteousness of saints."* Fine linen is the righteous deeds or acts of God's servants.

All of these saints will receive their rewards (crowns) at the Judgment Seat of Christ. She is now prepared for the Marriage Supper of the Lamb. The angel commands John to write, *"Blessed are they which are called unto the Marriage Supper of the Lamb."* The angel also tells John, *"These are the true sayings of God."* John falls at the angel's feet to worship him. Then the angel says to John, *"See thou do it not: I am thy fellowservant, and of thy brethren that have the testimony of Jesus: worship God: for the testimony of Jesus is the spirit of prophecy."*

Second Coming of Christ

Then John sees heaven open and beholds a rider sitting on a white horse. The rider is called Faithful and True and in righteousness, He does judge and makes war. His eyes were as a flame of fire and on His head were many crowns. He has a name written that no man knew but Himself. He is wearing a vesture dipped in blood. This event was prophesied in Isaiah 63:1-6 when

Chapter Nineteen

it says, *"Who is this that cometh from Edom, with dyed garments from Bozrah? This that is glorious in His apparel, travelling in the greatness of His strength? I that speak in righteousness, mighty to save. Wherefore art Thou red in Thine apparel, and Thy garments like Him that treadeth in the winefat? I have trodden the winepress alone; and of the people there was none with Me: for I will tread them in Mine anger, and trample them in My fury; and their blood shall be sprinkled upon My garments, and I will stain all My raiment. For the day of vengeance is in Mine heart, and the year of My redeemed is come. And I looked, and there was none to help; and I wondered that there was none to uphold: therefore Mine own arm brought salvation unto Me; and My fury, it upheld Me. And I will tread down the people in Mine anger, and make them drunk in My fury, and I will bring down their strength to the earth."* His name is called The Word of God. This is Jesus in all of His Restored Glory that He had in the beginning before the foundation of the world. John 17:4-5 says, *"I have glorified Thee on the earth: I have finished the work which Thou gavest Me to do. And now, O Father, glorify Thou Me with Thine Own Self with the Glory which I had with Thee before the world was."*

(For An Explanation of The Triune Godhead – See The Holy Trinity – The Triune God)

All of the nation of Israel will be saved at this time. The scripture says in Zechariah 12:10-11, *"And I will pour upon the house of David, and upon the inhabitants*

Chapter Nineteen

of Jerusalem, the spirit of grace and of supplications: and they shall look upon Me Whom they have pierced, and they shall mourn for Him, as one mourneth for his only son, and shall be in bitterness for Him, as one that is in bitterness for his firstborn. In that day shall there be a great mourning in Jerusalem, as the mourning of Hadadrimmon in the valley of Megiddon." According to Matthew 23:39, all of the nation of Israel will respond as Jesus said, *"For I say unto you, Ye shall not see Me henceforth, till ye shall say, Blessed is He that cometh in the name of the Lord"* The Lord God keeps His promises when He said in Hosea 6:1-3, *"Come, and let us return unto the Lord: for He hath torn, and He will heal us; He hath smitten, and He will bind us up. <u>After two days</u> will He revive us: in the <u>third day</u> He will raise us up, and we shall live in His sight. Then shall we know, if we follow on to know the Lord: His going forth is prepared as the morning; and He shall come unto us as the rain, as the latter and former rain unto the earth."*

The armies which were in heaven followed Him upon white horses, clothed in fine linen, white and clean. This army, clothed in fine linen, is the righteous saints and the fulfillment of prophecy in Colossians 3:4 which says, *"When Christ, Who is our Life, shall appear, then shall ye also appear with Him in glory"* (Zechariah 14:5). And in Matthew 25:31-34, 41 which says, *"When the Son of Man shall come in His glory, and all the holy angels with Him, then shall He sit upon the throne of His glory: And before Him shall be gathered all nations: and He shall separate them one from another, as a shepherd*

Chapter Nineteen

divideth His sheep from the goats: And He shall set the sheep on His right hand, but the goats on the left. Then shall the King say unto them on His right hand, Come, ye blessed of My Father, inherit the kingdom prepared for you from the foundation of the world...Then shall He say also unto them on the left hand, Depart from Me, ye cursed, into everlasting fire, prepared for the devil and his angels."

Out of His mouth proceeds a sharp sword which He uses to smite the nations. He will rule the nations with a rod of iron during His millennial kingdom reign (Revelation 2:7, 12:5; Psalm 2:9, 110:2; Isaiah 11:4). The scripture says that the Father judges no man but has given all judgment to the Son (John 5:22, 27). He treads the winepress of the fierceness and wrath of Almighty God. On His vesture and thigh is a name written, KING OF KINGS AND LORD OF LORDS.

Then John sees an angel standing in the sun and He cried with a loud voice saying to all the fowls that fly in the midst of heaven, *"Come and gather yourselves together unto the supper of the great God; That ye may eat the flesh of kings, and the flesh of captains, and the flesh of mighty men, and the flesh of horses, and of them that sit on them, and the flesh of all men, both free and bond, both small and great."* **Then, John sees the beast (Antichrist), the kings of the earth, and their armies gathering together to make war against Him that sat on the horse and against His army. The beast (Antichrist) was taken and the false prophet with him, who worked**

Chapter Nineteen

miracles before him with which he deceived the nations into receiving the mark of the beast and causing them to worship the Antichrist and the Antichrist's image, were both casts alive into a lake of fire burning with brimstone. The remnant was slain with the sword of Him that sat upon the horse Whose sword proceeded out of His mouth and all the fowls were filled with their flesh.

CHAPTER TWENTY

John sees an angel coming from heaven having the key of the bottomless pit and a great chain in his hand. The angel lays hold of the dragon, that old serpent, which is the Devil and Satan, and bound him a thousand years. He casts Satan into the bottomless pit and shut him up inside. He sets a seal upon him so that he will not deceive the nations anymore until the thousand years be fulfilled. After the thousand years are fulfilled, Satan is loosed for a little season.

Then, John sees thrones and those that sat upon them and judgment was given to them. He also sees the souls of them that were beheaded for the witness of Jesus and for the word of God who had worshipped neither the beast (Antichrist), nor his image, nor had they received his mark upon their foreheads or in their hands. They will live and reign with Christ for a

Chapter Twenty

thousand years. The rest of the dead did not live again until the thousand years were finished. This is the first resurrection. *"Blessed and holy is he that hath part in the first resurrection: on such the second death hath no power, but they shall be priests of God and of Christ, and shall reign with Him a thousand years."*

When the thousand years are expired, Satan will be loosed from his prison and will go out to deceive the nations which are in the four quarters of the earth, Gog and Magog. He will gather the nations together to battle. The nations will be as numerous as the sand of the sea. And they went up on the breadth or broad plain of the land and compassed the camp of the saints about in the beloved city (Jerusalem). Fire will come down from God out of heaven and devour them. The devil that deceived them will be cast into the lake of fire and brimstone where the beast (Antichrist) and the false prophet were cast. They will be tormented day and night forever and ever throughout eternity.

Now, John sees a great white throne and Him that sat on the throne from Whose face the current earth and heaven fled away and there was found no place for them. John also sees the dead, small and great, stand before God. The books were opened. And another book was opened, which is the Book of Life. The dead were judged out of those things which were written in the books and according to their works or deeds.

The sea will give up the dead which is in it. Death and hell will deliver up the dead which is in them. The dead will be judged according to their works. Matthew

Chapter Twenty

25:41 says, *"Then shall He say also unto them on the left hand, Depart from Me, ye cursed, into everlasting fire, prepared for the devil and his angels."* Death and hell will be cast into the lake of fire. This is the second death (eternal damnation) because whosoever name is not found written in the Book of Life will be cast into the lake of fire.

CHAPTER TWENTY ONE

New Heaven and a New Earth

John sees a new heaven and a new earth because the first heaven and the first earth were passed away. There was no sea. He sees the Holy City, New Jerusalem, coming down from God out of heaven prepared as a bride adorned for her husband. Then he hears a great voice out of heaven saying, *"Behold, the tabernacle of God is with men, and He will dwell with them, and they shall be His people, and God Himself shall be with them, and be their God. And God shall wipe away all tears from their eyes; and there shall be no more death, neither sorrow, nor crying, neither shall there be any more pain: for the former things are passed away."* He that sat upon the throne said, *"Behold, I make all*

Chapter Twenty One

things new." He said to John, *"Write: for these words are true and faithful."* He also said to John, *"It is done. I am Alpha and Omega, the Beginning and the End. I will give unto him that is athirst of the Fountain of The Water of Life freely. He that overcometh shall inherit all things; and I will be his God, and he shall be My son. But the fearful, and unbelieving, and the abominable, and murderers, and whoremongers, and sorcerers, and idolaters, and all liars, shall have their part in the lake which burneth with fire and brimstone: which is the second death."*

New Jerusalem

There came to John one of the seven angels which had the seven vials full of the seven last plagues and talked with him saying, *"Come hither, I will shew thee the bride, the Lamb's wife."* He carried John away in the spirit to a great and high mountain and showed him that great city, the holy Jerusalem, descending out of heaven from God having the glory of God. Her light was like a most precious stone, even like a jasper stone, clear as crystal. It has a great and high wall and twelve gates. At each of the twelve gates were twelve angels. The names of the twelve tribes of the children of Israel were written upon the gates. There are three gates in the east, three gates in the north, three gates in the south, and three gates in the west. The wall of the city had twelve foundations in which the names of the twelve apostles of the Lamb were written. The angel that spoke with John had a golden rod to measure the city, the gates, and the wall. The city is shaped like a square. He measured the city with the rod and it was twelve thousand furlongs (between 1380-1500 miles). The length, the width, and the height of the city are equal. He measured the wall and it was a hundred and forty-four cubits (216 feet) according to human standards of measurement with which the angel used to measure the wall. The wall was made of jasper. The city was pure gold like clear glass. The foundations of the wall of the city were garnished with all manner of precious stones. The first foundation was jasper; the second sapphire; the third a chalcedony; the fourth an emerald; the fifth sardonyx; the sixth sardius; the seventh chrysolyte; the eighth beryl; the ninth a topaz; the tenth a chrysoprasus; the eleventh a jacinth; the twelfth an amethyst. The twelve gates were made of twelve pearls. Each gate was made of one pearl. The street of the city was pure gold like transparent glass. John saw no temple in the city because the Lord God Almighty and the Lamb is its temple. The city had no need of the sun or the moon to shine on it because the glory of God lights up the city and the Lamb is the source of the light.

The nations which are saved shall walk in the light of it and the kings of the earth do bring their glory and honor into the city. The gates will not be shut but will remain open because there is no night. The nations will bring the glory and honor into the city. Nothing will enter into the city that defiles, or is an abomination, or lies. Only those whose names are written in the Lamb's Book of Life will enter into the city.

Chapter Twenty One

The Holy New Jerusalem that descends out of heaven from God having the glory of God is the permanent dwelling place for all of those whose names were written in the Lamb's Book of Life. The Lord God original intent will be established. It will be just like God intended our current heaven and earth to be prior to the serpent deceiving Eve and causing Adam to sin. The Tree of Life will be there. God Almighty and the Lamb will dwell in the midst of the people. There will be no need for the sun and the moon to give light. The Lamb of God shall light up the city for He is our Sun of Righteousness and shall shine like the white part of a fiery flame (Malachi 4:2; Daniel 7:9). The scripture says in Psalm 84:11, *"For the Lord God is a Sun and Shield: the Lord will give grace and glory: no good thing will He withhold from them that walk uprightly."* Peter, James, and John were eyewitnesses to His transfiguration when He took His mortal body and transformed it into a Sun and then back to a mortal body. Matthew 17:2 says, *"And was transfigured before them: and His face did shine as the sun, and His raiment was white as the light."* The inhabitants or people in the city will not remember the former heaven and earth or the former things because the Lord God never intended for man to have knowledge of good and evil.

CHAPTER TWENTY TWO

Then, he shows John a pure river of water of life, clear as crystal, proceeding out of the throne of God and of the Lamb. In the middle of the street and on either side of the river, was the Tree of Life which bears twelve different kinds of fruits and yields her fruit every month. The leaves of the tree were for the healing of the nations. There will be no more curse. The throne of God and of the Lamb shall be in it and His servants shall serve Him. They will see His face (1st Corinthians 13:12). His name will be in their foreheads (Revelation 7:3, 9:4, 14:1). There will be no night there and neither the need for a candle nor the light of the sun because the Lord God gives them light and they shall reign forever and ever.

Chapter Twenty Two

He said to John, *"These sayings are faithful and true: and the Lord God of the holy prophets sent His angel to shew unto His servants the things which must shortly be done."* Jesus said, *"Behold, I come quickly: blessed is he that keepeth the sayings of the prophecy of this book."* I, John, saw these things and heard them. When I had heard and seen, I fell down to worship before the feet of the angel which showed me these things. Then, he said to me, *"See thou do it not: for I am thy fellow servant, and of thy brethren the prophets, and of them which keep the sayings of this book: worship God."* Then, he said to me, *"Seal not the sayings of the prophecy of this book: for the time is at hand. He that is unjust, let him be unjust still: and he which is filthy, let him be filthy still: and he that is righteous, let him be righteous still: and he that is holy, let him be holy still."* Jesus said, *"Behold, I come quickly; and My reward is with Me, to give every man according as his work shall be. I am Alpha and Omega, the Beginning and the End, the First and the Last."* Blessed are they that do His commandments so that they may have a right to the Tree of Life and may enter in through the gates into the city. Outside are dogs, sorcerers, whoremongers, murderers, idolaters, and whosoever loves and practice lies. Jesus said, *"I, Jesus have sent Mine angel to testify unto you these things in the churches. I am the Root and the Offspring of David, and the Bright and Morning Star."* The Spirit and the bride say, *"Come."* Let him that hears say, *"Come."* Let him that is thirsty come. And whosoever will let him take of the water of life freely. I testify to every man that hears the words of the prophecy of this book

Chapter Twenty Two

that if any man shall add to these things, God will add to him the plagues that are written in this book. If any man shall take away from the words of the book of this prophecy, God shall take away his part out of the Book of Life and out of the holy city and from the things which are written in this book. He who testifies to these things said, *"Surely I come quickly."* Amen. Even so, come, Lord Jesus. The grace of our Lord Jesus Christ is with you all. Amen.

CONCLUSION

The book of Revelation is written to encourage the believer to hide the word of God in our heart and to live by every word that proceeds out of the mouth of God until He returns (Psalm 119:11; Matthew 4:4, 28:20). Therefore, let us remember what it says in Romans 8:28-30, *"And we know that all things work together for good to them that love God, to them who are the called according to His purpose. For whom He did foreknow, He also did predestinate to be conformed to the image of His Son, that He might be the firstborn among many brethren. Moreover whom He did predestinate, them He also called: and whom He called, them He also justified: and whom He justified, them He also glorified."*

The scripture lets us know in 1ˢᵗ Peter 2:9-10, *"But ye are a chosen generation, a royal priesthood, an holy nation, a peculiar people; that ye should shew forth the praises of Him who hath called you out of darkness into*

Conclusion

His marvellous light; Which in time past were not a people, but are now the people of God: which had not obtained mercy, but now have obtained mercy."

Jesus informs us in John 16:33, *"These things I have spoken unto you, that in Me ye might have peace In the world ye shall have tribulation: but be of good cheer; I have overcome the world."* He is just letting His followers know that there will be tribulations while we are here in the earth. Jesus encourages His believers (followers/disciples/church) in Matthew 24:6-14, *"And ye shall hear of wars and rumours of wars: see that ye be not troubled: for all these things must come to pass, but the end is not yet. For nation shall rise against nation, and kingdom against kingdom: and there shall be famines, and pestilences, and earthquakes, in diver's places. All these are the beginning of sorrows. Then shall they deliver you up to be afflicted, and shall kill you: and ye shall be hated of all nations for My name's sake. And then shall many be offended, and shall betray one another, and shall hate one another. And many false prophets shall rise, and shall deceive many. And because iniquity shall abound, the love of many shall wax cold. But he that shall endure unto the end, the same shall be saved. And this gospel of the kingdom shall be preached in all the world for a witness unto all nations; and then shall the end come."* According to the scriptures, tribulation is defined as a time of great sorrow, trouble, affliction, or suffering. However, there is hope. Apostle Peter lets us know in 1st Peter 5:10, *"But the God of all grace, Who hath called us unto His eternal glory by Christ Jesus, after that ye have suffered a while, make you perfect, stablish, strengthen, settle you."*

For example, in the book of Job chapters 1 and 2, the scripture tells us that Job was a perfect (blameless) and

Conclusion

upright man that feared (reverenced) God, and eschewed (shunned) evil. When the days of his son's feasting ceased, Job sent for his children and sanctified them early in the morning. He offered burnt offerings according to the number of them. Job said, *"It may be that my sons have sinned and cursed God in their hearts."* Job performed these offerings continually.

On two separate occasions when the sons of God came to present themselves to the Lord, Satan appeared also. Each time the Lord inquired of Satan's whereabouts and Satan's response was the same. *"From going to and fro in the earth, and from walking up and down in it."* Then, the Lord said to Satan, *"Hast thou considered My servant Job, that there is none like him in the earth, a perfect and an upright man, one that feareth God, and escheweth evil? Then Satan answered the Lord and said, Doth Job fear God for nought? Hast not Thou made an hedge about him, and about his house, and about all that he hath on every side? Thou hast blessed the work of his hands, and his substance is increased in the land. But put forth Thine hand now, and touch all that he hath, and he will curse Thee to thy face."*

The first time, the Lord's response to Satan was *"Behold, all that he hath is in thy power; only upon himself put not forth thine hand. So Satan went forth from the presence of the Lord."* And in one day, Satan caused all kinds of havoc in Job's life.

Each time there was a messenger to escape and tell Job. *"<u>The Sabeans</u> slain the servants with the edge of the sword and took away the oxen that were plowing and the asses feeding beside them."* While he was yet speaking, there came another and said, *"<u>The fire of God</u> is fallen*

Conclusion

from heaven, and hath burned up the sheep, and the servants, and consumed them." While he was yet speaking, there came also another and said, <u>The Chaldeans</u> made out three bands and fell upon the camels and have carried them away, yea, and slain the servants with the edge of the sword." While he was yet speaking, there came also another and said, "Thy sons and thy daughters were eating and drinking wine in their eldest brother's house: And, behold, there came <u>a great wind from the wilderness</u>, and smote the four corners of the house, and it fell upon the young men, and they are dead." The scripture tells us that *"Then Job arose, and rent his mantle, and shaved his head, and fell down upon the ground, and worshipped, And said, Naked came I out of my mother's womb, and naked shall I return thither: the Lord gave, and the Lord hath taken away; blessed be the name of the Lord. In all this Job sinned not, nor charged God foolishly."*

On the second occasion in Job chapter 2, the Lord asked Satan, *"Hast thou considered My servant Job, that there is none like him in the earth, a perfect and an upright man, one that feareth God, and escheweth evil? and still he holdeth fast his integrity, although thou movedst Me against him, to destroy him without cause. And Satan answered the Lord and said, Skin for skin, yea, all that a man hath will he give for his life. But put forth Thine hand now, and touch his bone and his flesh, and he will curse Thee to Thy face."*

This time the Lord's response to Satan was, *"Behold, he is in thine hand; but save his life."* Satan left the presence of the Lord and smote Job with sore boils from the sole of his foot to the crown of his head.

Conclusion

Job's wife said to him, *"Dost thou still retain thine integrity? curse God, and die."* He said to her, *"Thou speakest as one of the foolish women speaketh. What? shall we receive good at the hand of God, and shall we not receive evil?"* After all that Job suffered, he did not curse God by sinning with his lips.

Therefore, in chapter 42, the Lord gave Job twice as much as he had before because of Job's faithfulness and commitment to the Lord. Jesus reminds us to be steadfast in times of tribulations, sufferings, losses, and persecutions in Mark 10:29-30, *"And Jesus answered and said, Verily I say unto you, There is no man that hath left house, or brethren, or sisters, or father, or mother, or wife, or children, or lands, for My sake, and the gospel's, but he shall receive an hundredfold now in this time, houses, and brethren, and sisters, and mothers, and children, and lands, with persecutions; and in the world to come eternal life."*

Job's troubles were created because Satan wanted him to curse God. Job thought that his troubles and losses were because of "what he feared" or "was afraid of" from the hand of God (Job 2:10, 3:25). Job did not know that God and Satan had a private conversation about him to see if he would curse God if he was stripped of all his possessions, children, and health.

Just like Job, the tribulations and persecutions that we endure are not even about us. They are about the Lord. The battles we face are between the kingdom of good (light) and the kingdom of evil (darkness). Jesus said in John 7:7, *"The world cannot hate you; but Me it hateth, because I testify of it, that the works thereof are evil."* In John 15:18-21 Jesus said, *"If the world hate you, ye know that it hated Me before it hated you. If ye*

Conclusion

were of the world, the world would love his own: but because ye are not of the world, but I have chosen you out of the world, therefore the world hateth you. Remember the word that I said unto you, The servant is not greater than his lord. If they have persecuted Me, they will also persecute you; if they have kept My saying, they will keep yours also. But all these things will they do unto you for My name's sake, because they know not Him that sent Me."

Job's tribulations were to get him to curse God by attacking his possessions, his children, and his body. Satan even used those nearest to Job (his wife and friends) to persecute and add pressure to Job's weariness. One of Job's friend (Bildad) said in chapter 8:4, 20, *"If thy children have sinned against Him, and He have cast them away for their transgression;"* and *"Behold, God will not cast away a perfect man, neither will He help the evil doers."* God will not cast away a blameless (righteous man). However, He will allow him to be tried and tested by Satan in order to show His glory in the person being tested. Just like there was always one messenger to escape from the calamities and tell Job, God always will have a way of escape for the blameless (righteous). First Corinthians 10:13 says, *"There hath no temptation taken you but such as is common to man: but God is faithful, Who will not suffer you to be tempted above that ye are able; but will with the temptation also make a way to escape, that ye may be able to bear it."* Job had two other friends to offer their free counseling services. They vexed Job so much that Job called all three of them miserable comforters (Job 16:2). The Lord chastised all three of Jobs friends by telling them *"...My wrath is kindled against thee, and against thy two friends: for ye have not spoken of Me the thing that is right, as My servant Job hath"* (Job 42:7).

Conclusion

Peter tells us that Satan goes about like a roaring lion seeking whom he <u>may</u> devour. He continuously accuses us (the believers) before the Lord. He gets permission from the Lord to bring tribulations and persecutions in order to get a person to sin and curse (blaspheme) God in which he will be successful in doing during the great tribulation. Job said in Job 16:21, *"O that one might plead for a man with God, as a man pleadeth for his neighbour!"* How blessed we are! First Timothy 2:4-6 says, *"Who (God) will have all men to be saved, and to come unto the knowledge of the truth. For there is one God, and one mediator between God and men, the Man Christ Jesus; Who gave Himself a ransom for all, to be testified in due time."* Jesus is our Mediator. Guess what! There is coming a day when we will be forever with God, the Father. We will gain all that Adam lost in the Garden of Eden.

We as believers will be spared from the wrath to come (the great tribulation – Revelation 4:10). Satan persuaded the Lord to allow him to destroy all that Job had and to afflict Job's body without a cause. Job was not consumed by Satan because the Lord's wrath was not against Job. He said Job was without a cause or blameless. The Lord gave Satan certain restraints as to how far he could go in his attacks against Job. Remember that all of Job's attacks or losses were performed by Satan. Satan is the leviathan mention in Job 41:1-34 and no one can bind him, but the Lord God Almighty. If there were no restraints set by the Lord, Job would have been totally destroyed. The Lord is the restrainer that is mentioned in 2nd Thessalonians 2:6-7. According to Webster's Third New International Dictionary, the word "restrain" means to hold (as of a person) back from some action, procedure, or course; to keep within bounds or under control.

Conclusion

Examples of the Restrainer: *The Name of Jesus*

Philippians 2:9-11 (see also Romans 14:11-12)
⁹ *"Wherefore God also hath highly exalted Him, and given Him a name which is above every name:*
¹⁰ *That <u>at the name of Jesus every knee should bow, of things in heaven, and things in earth, and things under the earth;</u>*
¹¹ *And that every tongue should confess that Jesus Christ is Lord, to the Glory of God the Father."*

Jude 1:9
⁹ *"Yet Michael the archangel, when contending with the devil he disputed about the body of Moses, durst not bring against him a railing accusation, but said, <u>The Lord rebuke thee.</u>"*

For example, a police officer has been given delegated authority (badge) by the city which employs him. He has the authority to stop or pull over a person because the transgressor has transgressed against the law (for example, speeding). He has the right to restrain the transgressor or give a warning and let him go. Whatever decision he makes, within the confines of his jurisdiction, the police department that hired him will back him up.

Therefore, Jesus has been given authority and all judgment by God, the Father. It is at His name and command that things are restrained. He has given us power and authority to restrain the works of all devils when we say, "Satan, the Lord rebuke you" or "in the name of Jesus" (1st John 3:8; Luke 9:1-2). When we pray, we pray to the Father in the name of Jesus (John 14:13-14, 16:21-22). It is the Lord that rebukes Satan (Zechariah 3:1-2; Jude 1:9). Therefore, it is in the name

Conclusion

of the Lord (Jesus) that Satan and his fallen angels are rebuked or restrained.

Satan is the leviathan and the king over all the children of pride (Job 41:1-34; Isaiah 27:1). He first appears in the scripture as a serpent in the Garden of Eden and deceived Eve. His punishment for his deception is that he is cursed above all cattle, above every beast of the field, upon his belly shall he crawl, and dust shall he eat all the days of his (Genesis 3:14). The scripture tells us that the God resists the proud and we are to resist the devil (James 4:6-7). Nahum 1:2 says, *"God is jealous, and the Lord revengeth; the Lord revengeth, and is furious; the Lord will take vengeance on His adversaries, and He reserveth wrath for His enemies."*

Jesus satisfied the wrath of God by being sent to be the propitiation (atoning sacrifice) for our sins because the chastisement of our peace was upon Him (1st John 2:2, 4:10; Isaiah 53:5). The scripture says in the mouth of two or three witnesses shall every word be established. Here are two witnesses. First Thessalonians 1:10 says, *"And to wait for His Son from heaven, Whom He raised from the dead, even Jesus, which delivered us from the wrath to come."* First Thessalonians 5:9-10, *"For God hath not appointed us to wrath, but to obtain salvation by our Lord Jesus Christ, Who died for us, that, whether we wake or sleep, we should live together with Him."*

PRAYER OF SALVATION

If you are a sinner and want to make Jesus Christ your Savior and Lord, then all you have to do is believe on the Lord Jesus Christ and you are saved.

Pray aloud. Father God, in the name of Jesus, I am a sinner and I repent of all of my sins. I believe and confess that Jesus died for my sins by shedding His blood, on the cross, at Calvary and rose three days later from the grave for my justification. Father, give me a new heart and be my Lord forever. In Jesus' name. Amen.

Salvation is just that simple. You are saved and have eternal life in Christ Jesus no matter what Satan or any other person tells you. All of your sins (past, present, and future) are forgiven by the blood of Jesus and you are justified by Jesus as if you never sinned (blameless).

PRAYER FOR THE BAPTISM WITH THE HOLY GHOST

After praying the prayer of salvation, pray. Father God, You said in Your word, "If we, being evil, know how to give good gifts to our children, how much more shall our Father, Who is in heaven, give good things to them that ask Him?" Therefore, Lord, endow me with the power of the Holy Ghost and with the evidence of speaking in other tongues. I thank You and receive my heavenly language. In Jesus' name. Amen.

www.ingramcontent.com/pod-product-compliance
Lightning Source LLC
Chambersburg PA
CBHW071155070526
44584CB00019B/2800